THE 2-HOUR WORKSHOP BLUEPRINT

DESIGN FAST.
DELIVER STRONG.
WITHOUT STRESS.

By
Leanne Hughes

VIDEO SUMMARY

Read This First

Want a video summary of this book that will help you start making progress on YOUR workshop quickly?

Check out this video training and overview of the process.

In this training I cover three things:

1. **How to rapidly turn your content into a workshop framework**

2. **How to give precise instructions for your activities**

3. **How to book more workshops**

2HOURWORK.SHOP/VIDEO

"With this road-tested toolkit, you will learn exactly how to design and deliver memorable workshops in a fraction of the time, spreading that same gold dust of contagious energy that Leanne herself so brilliantly brings into the world."
- Jenny Blake, Co-creator of Google's Career Guru program and author of Free Time, Pivot, and Life After College

"Good content, bad design and facilitation? Death. OK content, great design and facilitation? Glory. Leanne Hughes is the perfect guide, and in this book she lays down the foundations for your workshop success."
— Michael Bungay Stanier, bestselling author of The Coaching Habit and How to Work with (Almost) Anyone

"In this clever book, Leanne Hughes takes you through the creation and delivery of workshops with alacrity and passion. You'll learn how to attract and engage participants, deliver solid content that's immediately applicable, and evaluate your own progress. You can't read a book to learn how to ski. But you can read this book and learn how to create brilliant workshops."
— Alan Weiss, PhD, author, Million Dollar Consulting, Sentient Strategy, and over 50 other books

"As someone who has spent years studying the art of communication, I can say with confidence that Leanne's book is a valuable resource for anyone looking to improve their workshop design and hosting skills."
— Jordan Harbinger, creator, The Jordan Harbinger Show

"Leanne Hughes' advice is smart, punchy, actionable and BS-free - just like the workshops she will help you to design and deliver. If you want to level up your facilitation game, start here!"
— Leslie Ehm, bestselling author of Swagger, and founder of Combustion Training

"Pay attention to Leanne's book, filled with practical advice you can apply when you need to facilitate a workshop that is interactive, energetic, and engaging."
— Neen James, executive strategist, author of Attention Pays

"Backed by her extensive experience and insights from over 200 podcast interviews, this book is an essential companion for anyone who wants to create impactful workshops without getting entangled in the complexities of facilitation. It will quickly become your go-to resource for crafting informative, engaging, and unforgettable workshop experiences."
— Dr Myriam Hadnes, host of the Workshops Work podcast and NeverDoneBefore community

"If you're looking for a practical guide to creating workshops that truly resonate with your audience, Leanne's book is a must-read, making it easy to turn your expertise into a memorable and effective workshop experience."
— Pat Flynn, Co-founder of SPI Media & Author of Bestselling books Superfans and Will it Fly

"This is the book I wish I had read when I started developing workshops, many years ago. Leanne makes workshop development sound easy - and that's because it can be. It's a must-read for facilitators, trainers and teachers, especially if you're an over-thinker who spends far too long re-working everything so it's "just right"... — **Mel Kettle, Leadership Communication Strategist, Speaker, Author, Facilitator**

"What sets this book apart from others on the same topic is the abundance of little pearls of wisdom that are sprinkled throughout. These insights are practical, actionable, and make the process of designing a workshop feel less overwhelming." — **Kerry Brocks, CEO & founder, Institute for Learning & Performance**

"If you want to overcome the fear of rejection, there's no better way than getting in front of a group of people and sharing your message. Leanne's book provides a valuable resource for anyone looking to do just that, with practical tips and strategies for delivering a workshop that inspires change." — **Jia Jiang, author Rejection Proof and TED Speaker: What I learned from 100 days of rejection**

Big Charlie Press

The 2-Hour Workshop Blueprint

Design Fast. Deliver Strong. Without Stress.

Copyright © 2023 Leanne Hughes

ISBN: 978-0-6457400-0-4 (paperback)

ISBN: 978-0-6457400-1-1 (ebook)

ISBN: 978-0-6457400-2-8 (audio)

Dedicated to my co-facilitators in the sky:

Charlie Opu Foisape and Alwyn Hughes.

CONTENTS

CHAPTER ONE

What this book's about, how it can help you, plus a quick hello

Welcome to this punchy guide to designing and delivering impactful, short group workshops in a fraction of the time. As you read (or, like I usually do, skim!) through these pages, you'll learn how to share your expertise and build group engagement quickly and easily.

I'll show you how to use my proven workshop blueprint to avoid spending countless hours searching for the perfect activity for your upcoming session.

THIS BOOK IS YOUR COMPANION GUIDE

Designing workshops just got easier.

This book is perfect for you if:

- You want to turn your knowledge, expertise, wisdom, and insights into an exciting workshop experience.

- You're seeking ideas on how to keep your group engaged every step of the way.

- You have a clear understanding of your target audience and want to create a workshop that meets their needs.

You can use this workshop blueprint for delivering two-hour workshops on anything training, teaching, or content-related; ranging from data analysis and visualisation tips, to sharing your favourite dog-grooming techniques.

However, it's not intended for those seeking guidance on designing *process-type* workshops like strategy sessions or design sprints.

- While you may find some helpful ideas on how to prepare and deliver these types of session, the focus is on creating two-hour workshops that showcase your expertise and connect with your audience.

BE REALISTIC ABOUT THE OUTCOME

Disclaimer: While a two-hour session can build awareness, share ideas, and help people progress, it cannot achieve major culture shifts or eliminate unconscious bias. Workshops can help but they need to be part of a bigger process, to achieve real business outcomes.

HOW TO USE THIS BOOK

I suggest reading from start to finish. It's short, and the concepts build on each other. But if you'd prefer to skip around, in the following Acts you'll find everything you need to design your two-hour workshop using the SPARK framework (more on that later…) including:

- Act I: Define the outcomes and focus on the destination of your workshop through three chapters.

- Act II: Map out your pre-start, opening, and the bulk of your workshop. Use questions, ideas, and activities to engage your participants.

- Act III: Put the finishing touches on your workshop design by identifying closing questions and activities. Develop strategies to communicate value to your participants after the workshop is over.

At the beginning of each chapter, you'll find a high-level overview of what's to come. As you complete a chapter, you're invited to review what you've learned through the Checkpoint prompts.

Explore the Helpful Extras section, at the back, to grab my workshop-hosting shopping list, and for extra tips on managing group behaviour, how to transition between workshop topics, and more.

Hope you enjoy the format! I was inspired to write it this way after reading Nick Gray's book, *The 2-Hour Cocktail Party* (hint: If you want to host a great party after your workshop to celebrate, grab his book!)

All the resources and digital tools mentioned in this book are available at 2hourwork.shop/freebies.

HOW I LEARNED TO DESIGN NON-BORING WORKSHOPS

Hi, my name is Leanne Hughes.

I've been working in corporate environments since 2007. In other words, I've sat through a lot of corporate presentations, team-building events, and workshop days. There were the ones that made the day drag on and on: PowerPoint slide after PowerPoint slide. So many corporate buzzwords. Everybody thinking, when's lunch?

Then occasionally, you'd get a surprise: a fantastic facilitator who energised the room and made you actually want to pump your fist in the air. Those were the ones you'd talk about afterwards!

In 2013, I volunteered to run a workshop for a local Shire Council in remote Western Australia. After that experience, I was hooked on leading these discussions and sharing skills in group settings.

I used to struggle with endlessly editing and reworking my workshop designs. It would often take me weeks to design a two-hour session. I would agonise over the icebreaker, question if the content was right, and try to figure out how to make it come alive. But with hundreds of group sessions, both in-person and online, I've learned the critical ingredients for creating engaging and practical workshops.

Now, when I design workshops, I step away from the computer. Instead of clicking through PowerPoint, I capture my ideas and structure on paper. It's joyful! I'd love to share that joy with you because workshop design should be a fun experience, not something you dread.

I'm really into personal development (I studied business and psychology), so I started working to be more like the workshop hosts I loved. People who saw my presentations began asking me for tips. Accountants and engineers would come to me with their material and ask, "Hey, how can I make this more interesting?" In case you can't tell, I love this stuff. I love it when people show up for 'just another boring training day' and it's not what they expect! I love turning their day around and surprising them with a really good time. I love seeing people actually learn a lot and have an amazing experience.

I've shared my expertise with clients from engineering firms to government departments. I have even taken my facilitation skills to places like Mongolia, Canada, Papua New Guinea, Singapore, France, and Australia.

I'm always looking for ways to improve. That's why I started my podcast, *First Time Facilitator*, where I've hosted over 200 conversations on workshop design and facilitation.

Join me on my journey to make workshop design more straightforward and more effective for you.

If you'd like to say hello, I'm hello@leannehughes.com or @leannehughes on Instagram and Twitter. I'm also active on LinkedIn, and I'd love to connect with you. You're also welcome to join my free Facebook community called *The Flipchart*, where we gather to share workshop ideas so that we can stamp out boring workshops worldwide forever.

WHY TWO-HOUR WORKSHOPS?

A two-hour workshop is the perfect starting point for learning how to design practical and engaging sessions. You cover it all in a two-hour session: You need to start strong, get involvement, and then close it off. The skills and principles shared here can be applied to any workshop, whether online or in person. I'll give you examples in this book for both.

In today's fast-paced world, people are time-poor and may struggle to commit to full-day workshops. A one to three-hour workshop is the perfect way to start applying these skills and making an impact.

You don't have to sacrifice quality for time; you can still make a tremendous impact in just a couple of hours.

That said, I've had people attend my *2-Hour Workshop Masterclass* program, and they've used the tools and philosophies in this book for their one- and two-day sessions and had immense success.

YOU CAN DO THIS!

Hosting workshops and creating a fantastic group experience is something that can be learned. None of us is born a facilitator or trainer; we all find our way to this role through different paths and backgrounds. This is a very practical guide, and my aim is to help you put your great ideas into practice easily.

Of course, there may be some bumps along the way as you start hosting your workshops or training sessions. I've had my share of mishaps, like when I was booted off my Zoom call or when I kept saying "pens down!" at the end of every activity until someone in the room was ready to throw a pen at me!

You've got this! But remember, even the most experienced facilitators make mistakes. The important thing is to learn from them and keep moving forward.

CHECKPOINT

- Are you delivering a workshop in the next 90 days? If so, what's it about? Send me an email hello@leannehughes. com and give me the scoop!

- Visit 2hourwork.shop/freebies to grab all your resources. We'll work through them as we progress through the chapters.

Let's get started!

CHAPTER TWO

Seven Practices of
Highly Effective Workshop Hosts

CHAPTER SUMMARY

*T*he *2-Hour Workshop Blueprint* has been carefully crafted with key philosophies in mind to make your workshop design experience seamless and impactful.

To give you a head start, I've gathered my top *Seven Practices of Highly Effective Workshop Hosts*. These tips will help you accelerate trust, start the conversation early, and bring your session to life with various techniques.

Whether you're hosting a virtual workshop or an in-person session, a short or an extended workshop, these habits will help you create a memorable experience for your participants.

THE SEVEN PRACTICES

1. Begin with the experience in mind.

2. Mix it up: Weave variety into your workshop to win attention.

3. Build the buzz: Get your groups showing up ready, invested, and active.

4. Master brevity: Be succinct and have faith in your audience's abilities.

5. Lead the energy: Direct the atmosphere of the workshop instead of reacting to it.

6. Iron your shirt the night before: Control the controllable, conquer the unexpected.

7. On time, every time: End sessions when scheduled (or even a minute earlier for bonus points).

PRACTICE #1: BEGIN WITH THE EXPERIENCE IN MIND

Workshops are not just about delivering information. With the abundance of information readily available online, simply sharing information is no longer enough to justify holding a workshop. Instead, the focus should be on creating a meaningful experience for participants, fostering interaction and engagement, and building connections among the group.

A workshop should aim to be more than just a lecture or presentation; it should be an immersive experience that offers context relevant to the specific needs of the participants. Too often, workshops are held because we don't trust that participants will read an email, follow a Slack channel, or watch a recorded video. It's convenient to invite a group of people together, but that's not a good enough reason to run a session. The value of a workshop lies in the experience you create, the relationships formed, and the personalised takeaways that participants leave with.

Many roads lead to the same destination

Let's say you're a tourist in New York City. You're staying near Rockefeller Center and want to visit a new restaurant in the West Village. There are dozens of different ways you could take to get there. You could taxi, Uber, cycle, or take the subway. You could walk there via the Flatiron building to take a photo or take a more scenic route via The High Line.

It depends on what experience you want to create on the way there:

- Do you want to get there quickly?

- Are you needing to get your exercise and daily step count up?

- Do you want to try a new mode of transport?

- Are there some great things to see on the way?

- Do you want to save money?

It's the same destination, right? But there are many ways to arrive. Like our workshops, we can drive a result, but we might do it differently. To help decide which route to take, you must consider the experience you want to create.

Design for the experience

Knowing the experience you want to create, including the atmosphere, engagement, and overall feel of your session, helps you decide where and how to host it. My friend and host of the *Steph's Business Bookshelf* podcast, Steph Clarke, shared an example. One of her clients wanted to think about the future in their strategy workshop, but they wanted to hold it in their old, dark boardroom. See the irony here? Steph responded to the client, suggested hosting their session in an environment that reflected the outcome: If you want blue sky thinking, head outdoors, or book a room with high ceilings and natural light streaming through.

PRACTICE #2: MIX IT UP: WEAVE VARIETY INTO YOUR WORKSHOP TO WIN ATTENTION

Shake things up to keep your group engaged and interested. You can't overestimate the importance of contrast. When I'm designing a conference or workshop, I'll use contrast as my litmus test. I'll look at the agenda, planned activities, and environment to ensure there's contrast across those areas. If there is too much 'sameness', I'll incorporate something else to mix it up. A video. A story. An activity where they need to build something physically. Write something down. Share through drawing. It's about changing the pace.

The five and one rule: Speak for no more than five minutes without introducing some contrast or giving someone else the chance to speak.

I always try to follow my five and one rule when facilitating a workshop. That means I aim to speak for no more than five minutes without introducing some contrast or giving someone else a chance to speak. Use contrast strategically to create an immersive and dynamic workshop experience that keeps your audience engaged, focused, and interested. Win, win, win.

PRACTICE #3: BUILD THE BUZZ: GET YOUR GROUPS SHOWING UP READY, INVESTED, AND ACTIVE.

Get straight to it: Skip the housekeeping; start with involvement. This rule has been lifted and modified from *The Art of Gathering* by Priya Parker. Parker's rule is 'Never start a funeral with logistics', and she shares: "Before your event starts, it has begun. Your gathering begins the moment your guest first learns of it. Your guests have been thinking about, preparing for, and anticipating your gathering well before that moment. The window of time between the discovery and the formal beginning is an opportunity to prime your guests."

Think about your group and how they will prepare for the workshop before it has even started. Do they have the right level of detail and information? What expectations are being set? What signals are you sending to your group that is helping to build anticipation and involvement?

As workshop hosts, your role does not simply start at the beginning of your workshop, so the setup is key. Instead of waiting to get involvement, start conversations earlier. How can you get your groups to feel excited about your session?

PRACTICE #4. MASTER BREVITY: BE SUCCINCT AND HAVE FAITH IN YOUR AUDIENCE'S ABILITIES.

Alan Weiss, the author of *Million Dollar Consulting*, says it best: "Tell them what they need to know, <u>not everything you know</u>." It's easy to fall into the trap of overloading our workshops with content, facts, data, activities, and stories. But the key to a successful workshop is choosing wisely what to include and to be ruthless with what you leave out.

I've been guilty of this many times: Overloading my workshop with too much content, facts, data, activities, or stories. I can tell you, it can lead to information overload and disengagement. This isn't a keynote speech: It's not a platform for you to showcase your brilliance and knowledge; rather it's an opportunity to inspire connection to the content.

> *More information doesn't always equal more value.*

Remember, more information doesn't always equal more value. I've been in workshops where things have been over-explained and I feel like saying, *"Hey, we get it already!"* Your participants are smart and can connect the dots without you explicitly doing it for them.

Focus on forming connections between group members and their relationship to the topic. Regularly check in to ensure they are with you. And be mindful of repeating information—the key is to keep your workshop streamlined and focused on delivering results.

PRACTICE #5. LEAD THE ENERGY: DIRECT THE ATMOSPHERE OF THE WORKSHOP INSTEAD OF REACTING TO IT.

Your enthusiasm can set the tone and be the driving force behind the success of your session. When I spoke with Mark Bowden, a world-renowned body language expert on the *First Time Facilitator* podcast, he shared that it can be challenging to understand your participants' body language and emotions collectively. However, he emphasised that the biggest predictor of group engagement is how energised YOU are!

I've seen this play out in workshops where I thought someone was disengaged due to their body language (you know what it's like: frowning, crossed arms), but then they approached me after the session, expressing how much they learned and how impactful the workshop was for them.

Lead by example and show your excitement and passion for the content you're sharing. Your energy and enthusiasm will be contagious, creating a positive learning environment.

Remember, if you're not invested in the content you're presenting, it's unlikely your group will be either.

PRACTICE #6. IRON YOUR SHIRT THE NIGHT BEFORE: CONTROL THE CONTROLLABLE, CONQUER THE UNEXPECTED

Ironing your shirt the night before is both a metaphor and has literal connotations, too. Prior to hosting a conference down on the Gold Coast, Australia, I had the most relaxing morning: going for a run and swanning around at breakfast. I went back to my hotel room to get ready, and when I put my shirt on, I realised there was a massive tear in it. Luckily, I had a backup shirt.

Facilitation, and life, in general, is unpredictable. But, by controlling the controllable, you'll be setting yourself up for success and a good night's sleep. Write your to-do list and check your calendar the night before to hit the ground running and make your day a success. It's a gift to your future self.

Sort out what you need before your session, so you can focus on being present with your group and not fiddling around with slides five minutes before your session begins.

PRACTICE #7. ON TIME, EVERY TIME: END SESSIONS WHEN SCHEDULED (OR EVEN A MINUTE EARLIER FOR BONUS POINTS)

This rule isn't about the timing so much, as it's about delivering on what you've promised, which is the best way to develop trust: the golden currency of workshop hosting. If there's an agenda and agreed-upon times, you're breaking a promise or a rule if the workshop or meeting time goes over. Your workshop is over when your two hours are up, which should be respected.

This also relates to starting on time. We've all been there, hosting a workshop and an 'important person' (i.e. someone higher in the org chart) hasn't arrived yet. It's tempting to wait for that person. But to set the right standard, you need to start that meeting on time. If you don't, you're telling the people who arrived at the workshop on time that they're not as important, or that it's okay to show up late to your sessions.

I learned this lesson firsthand with my 'Five Minute Rule'. I had a client who was late for our Zoom call, but I stuck to my rule and logged off after five minutes. This resulted in the client showing up two minutes early for our rescheduled session. Win!

These *Seven Practices for Highly Effective Workshop Hosts* apply to both virtual and in-person sessions of any length.

CASE STUDY

Here's an example of how my client, Amanda Moody, Associate Vice-President of the Planetree Institute, used these concepts to overhaul their multi-day workshop:

The challenge: For more than 30 years, Sun River Health has required all staff to participate in a foundational culture workshop called the Planetree Retreat. The intention of this workshop, which routinely takes place in person over two full days, is to connect staff to the history of community health centres, to the organisation's unique journey within this history, and to their reasons for pursuing a career in community health.

As more remote workers joined the organisation, some were out of state and unable to travel to participate in in-person workshops. We knew the time had come to adapt our workshop for a virtual audience.

The approach:

Firstly, they approached this revamp by beginning with the **experience in mind**. They convened a team of key staff and some health centre patients to consider how best to recreate the workshop aims in a virtual setting. They asked questions like, "How can we develop an atmosphere of connection and intimacy via Zoom?" They knew it could be done, but the stakes were very high for this program, the longest-running in the organisation's history.

Remembering that **content isn't everything**, they considered how certain activities would lend themselves to a virtual method and others would not. They reviewed the workshop curriculum, eliminating some activities and sessions, reviewing others, and adding new sessions that would better enable them to meet the aims by leveraging technology.

Emphasising **contrast**, they designed various activities, from group discussions to scavenger hunts, supporting various learning styles and getting folks up and moving throughout the day.

Finally, remembering that the session begins well before anyone logs into Zoom, they thoroughly planned for the **Before Session** period. To address potential engagement barriers related to technology, they connected all interested staff with the IT department in advance of the session to test their devices and connectivity.

Boxes were mailed to every participant that included all the supplies needed for the session activities, plus snacks and fidget toys. Finally, they also provided every participant with a gift card for a food delivery service to continue the practice of sharing a meal, even though participants were joining the meeting from different physical locations.

To prepare the facilitators to present in a virtual setting, they led a preparatory workshop on the importance of **'Leading the Room'** versus 'Reading the Room' and how facilitator energy levels, charisma, and skills generally needed to be adapted, not only to a new curriculum but to this new modality as well.

The Result:

Happily, Amanda can report that the virtual workshop provided a unique and no less meaningful experience for all participating staff. Session evaluations were particularly encouraging in the areas they had intentionally prioritised, such as the contrast between activities, and participants overwhelmingly agreed that the session's aims were achieved.

CHECKPOINT

As you read through the practices, mark down:

- Which practice are you strongest at?

- Which practice do you need a little help incorporating?

Strength	Improve	Practice
☐	☐	Begin with the experience in mind.
☐	☐	Mix it up: Weave variety into your workshop to win attention.
☐	☐	Build the buzz: Get your groups showing up ready, invested, and active.
☐	☐	Master brevity: Be succinct and have faith in your audience's abilities.
☐	☐	Lead the energy: Direct the atmosphere of the workshop instead of reacting to it.
☐	☐	Iron your shirt the night before: Control the controllable, conquer the unexpected.
☐	☐	On time, every time: End sessions when scheduled (or even a minute earlier for bonus points).

CHAPTER THREE

Accepting the Challenge:
SPARK Your 2-Hour Workshop Adventure

CHAPTER SUMMARY

Let me introduce you to the SPARK framework, a process for designing and delivering engaging and compelling workshops. The SPARK framework stands for Setup, Power Up, Activities, Review and Keep and is a linear path that guides workshop hosts through the process of turning their content and expertise into a successful workshop experience.

YOU'LL ALSO LEARN THE FOLLOWING:

- The importance of backstage activities: Why it's critical to prepare well before the workshop (Setup) and how to wrap it up after the workshop (Keep) for a successful experience.

- Time allocation for centre stage activities: Identify the general flow of a two-hour workshop and the time allocation for each centre stage activity (Power Up, Activities and Review).

YOU RECEIVE A CALL AND SPARK INTO ACTION

As we work through each element of the SPARK framework, we'll be applying it to a fictional scenario, where I (the workshop host) am approached by Bob, a General Manager in a supply chain team.

Here's where the scenario begins.

It's Wednesday afternoon, and I get a call from Bob, General Manager at Milo & Quincey Technologies.

"Hey, Leanne, our team is getting swamped. We have two hours set aside next Tuesday for our team meeting, but we're struggling to complete our meeting items from the last session. We must focus on determining how we'll get moving on certain tasks and what's getting in our way. We need your help.

Can you come run a workshop for us?"

I check my calendar; I love running these sessions. So, I move things around and accept Bob's request.

You might receive similar calls asking for your help. Or you might decide one day that instead of attending workshops, you think you can deliver one. Either way, you're going about your daily activities, and an opportunity emerges.

The opportunity could be a chance to:

- Share your expertise at a conference.

- Host a breakfast or webinar event to promote your great work.

- Provide information to new starters at your organisation.

- Capture project lessons learned and share them for an upcoming lunch and learn session.

- Teach a great skill you've picked up.

If you say YES (and good on you!), the next thing to do is to SPARK into action.

SPARK is a framework I created to design and deliver punchy sessions. Follow SPARK to turn your ideas and expertise, into a dynamic and meaningful workshop for your group.

SPARK FRAMEWORK

 SETUP

 POWER UP

 ACTIVITIES

 REVIEW

 KEEP

As you work through this book, you'll become familiar with each element and discover how they work together to bring your workshop to life. Under each phase of the framework, you'll find specific tools, activities and even scripts or questions that I use.

Also, SPARK is a great word, as that's what we aim to do in our workshops, right? Spark unique insights and connections, spark meaningful conversations, and spark some learning moments.

Let's create an all-round spark-tacular experience!

Okay, enough of the pep talk. Let's return to the framework…

Here are all the stages you'll work through as you turn your content and expertise into a fantastic group experience.

- **Setup:** Get clarity on who will be attending and the type of experience you want to create. Curate your content meaningfully and connect with your group before the workshop begins.

- **Power Up**: Kick off the workshop and get the energy flowing. Set the tone and expectations for the session and engage participants in the topic with interactive icebreakers and energisers.

- **Activities**: Design engaging activities and exercises that align with the workshop's goals. Encourage participation and facilitate discussion to enhance learning, immersion, and engagement.

- **Review:** Reflect on what was learned during the workshop and allow participants to process and internalise the information. Conduct debriefs, discuss next steps, and provide feedback. Evaluate your performance as a workshop host.

• **Keep:** Follow up with participants after the workshop and provide resources to continue the conversation. Reflect on the workshop's successes and areas for improvement. Save and store away successful activities for future workshops.

BACKSTAGE AND CENTRE STAGE

Hosting a workshop requires you to work both backstage (design) and centre stage (delivery) roles.

Hosting a workshop requires you to work both backstage and centre stage roles.

BACKSTAGE COMPONENTS

Both the S (Setup) and K (Keep) of the SPARK framework are backstage roles.

You do these things before or after your workshop to prepare and wrap up your session. They bookend your workshop. For a two-hour workshop, I prefer to start the Setup around two weeks prior. However, I've also delivered two-hour sessions with less than a day's notice. You don't want to be around me when that happens; just ask my husband, Chris.

In the Helpful Extras section, you'll find a checklist and suggested timings if you only have two hours to deliver a session.

For the Keep segment, I strongly suggest sending out workshop information and resources within 24 hours of your workshop finishing. To make this happen quickly, predict what resources you may share with participants and set up a simple website/link before the session.

CENTRE STAGE COMPONENTS

The P (Power Up), A (Activities), and R (Review) segments relate to delivering your workshop.

Let's say your two-hour workshop starts at 9 am. Here's the general flow of how you'll spend your time:

- Access the room 30-60 minutes earlier, if possible.

- Power Up: 50 minutes (8.30 am - 9.20 am)

- Activities: 75 minutes (9.20 am - 10.35 am)

- Review: 25 minutes (10.35 am – 11.00 am)

If you host virtual workshops, you might want to sneak in a five-to-seven-minute break. For in-person sessions, two hours without a break is fine.

BOB'S WORKSHOP: HIGH LEVEL SPARK EXAMPLE

In each chapter, we'll explore in greater detail how these elements work and how to create your own session. No need to worry if some of these words don't make sense just yet.

Before the session

Setup: Find out why Bob wants this session, what he's noticing and ask him to describe what success looks like (what his team members will be doing differently if the workshop is successful). Using this conversation as a base, draft topic ideas and sort these ideas under three key categories.

During the session

Power Up: Have the room ready 15 minutes before the session starts. Ask a couple of questions to help the group figure out their baseline and what areas they need to focus on. Playback key conversation themes to discover which are most poignant/resonant for them today.

Virtual session: Log onto the Zoom call earlier, test the technology and ensure my camera is on when participants arrive. Start engaging with participants immediately, for example I might throw a question into Chat to get the conversation started.

Activities: Using the three key categories, create three activities and discussion points to learn the topics and connect with them.

Virtual session: Use the Breakout Room feature only once, maybe twice and ask the group to participate in the session in various ways like chat, reactions, and unmuting their audio.

Reflection: Ask the group to reflect on their key insights and identify their path forward based on the three key categories shared in the workshop.

After the session

Keep: Share a link to resources and insights from the session.

HERE'S HOW WORKSHOP DESIGN CAN LOSE THE SPARK

If you're reading this, you might be in the same camp as me occasionally, and procrastinate over your workshop design: Endlessly tweaking content, getting new ideas, having to listen to every podcast about the topic before even thinking about sitting down to design it.

Before we leap in and start on the Setup phase, here are some tips that helped me move faster and stop overthinking the design component.

WE TAKE TOO MUCH TIME TO PLAN BECAUSE WE HAVE A LONG RUNWAY

Newsflash: more time to plan doesn't always equal a better experience. It's easy to get caught up in the details and spend a lot of time perfecting everything. But the truth is, having a long lead time doesn't necessarily mean your workshop will be better. At a certain point, those little adjustments just aren't worth it.

Tip: Say YES to delivering workshops where you have little notice. Follow this guide to make it impactful.

NOT FOCUSING ENOUGH ON RESULTS

We often fill our workshops with stories, activities, and data that don't align with the desired outcome for our group. Instead, be ruthless about what stays in and what goes out. Remember why your workshop exists and how it will serve your target audience, then work backwards to make it happen.

THE STAKES ARE HIGH

We worry about being 'good enough' and meeting the expectations of our participants, especially when the stakes are high. This pressure can come from various factors, such as the group we are working with or the amount of money we are being paid (a higher fee can make us feel like we must deliver more).

I'll help you overcome these challenges using SPARK and provide alternative solutions for each example.

Remember, you're awesome, and not many people step up to host workshops.

So take a deep breath, give me a high five, and let's get started!

CHECKPOINT

- Reflect on the last workshop or meeting you facilitated. Identify one area from the SPARK framework that could have improved the experience.

- Practice the Power Up stage for a workshop in a low-stakes environment, such as a team meeting or family gathering.

ACT

I

S for Setup is the first stage of your SPARK
process. Across three chapters, you'll start thinking
about the value your workshop offers and how
you can be more like a GPS focused on your
group's destination.

CHAPTER FOUR

S is for Setup

CHAPTER SUMMARY

In this chapter, you'll start thinking about the value your workshop offers and how you can define the outcomes.

DO:

- Identify your audience (who).

- Get clear on the results of your session (why).

- Invest the time upfront to curate your content (how).

DON'T:

- Go down a rabbit hole searching the web for everything related to your content:

YOU'LL WALK AWAY WITH THE FOLLOWING:

- A completed workshop mini-mission statement.

- A template you can use to design all your workshops.

When I first started delivering workshops, I didn't have a Setup stage. And if I did, it probably would have looked like this:

- Open PowerPoint.

- Visit Google and search for my topic.

- Cut and paste interesting information across slides.

- Edit, delete, move things around.

- Add some fun photos and videos.

- Deliver.

Sound familiar? This wasn't so bad, but what emerged was a mess: Lots of great content and information but no natural flow. It also meant I had to sit at the computer to design my sessions. Now, I find the best ideas are captured away from the screen.

THREE STEPS TO START YOUR WORKSHOP DESIGN

To capture that flow and make sure your workshop hits the mark, I suggest starting with these three steps:

1. Get clear on your workshop's purpose.

2. Create your 2-Hour Workshop Mini-Mission Statement.

3. Highlight three key topic areas as focus for your content.

Of all the SPARK steps, Setup is the most time-consuming.

However, it's worth the investment in energy and focus for many reasons:

- Improves the group experience: A carefully-planned workshop leads to increased participation and positive outcomes, plus boosts your brand and credibility, leading to future opportunities (no pressure!)

- Saves time and cuts out rework: Avoids the last-minute scramble and reducing the likelihood of problems or delays during the workshop.

- Increases efficiency: A well-planned workshop helps to optimise the use of resources, such as time, money, and materials.

- You'll get a better night's sleep.

REVAMP YOUR APPROACH: THE EXPERIENCE MATTERS MORE THAN YOUR CONTENT

No matter your topic, you're going to find hundreds of thousands of pieces of relevant content online. Many generic business-related workshops cover topics like Time Management, Leadership, Communication, etc. Search for any of these terms and you'll see millions of search results.

There are so many resources at our fingertips, yet you still receive a workshop request. Why is that?

*Your guiding question: What's most helpful and valuable for this group **right now?***

Remember Practice #1? It's not because your groups need more information or content. Workshops are no longer just about the content. A guiding question I use for every event is this: *What's most helpful and valuable for this group right now?* That's a question Google or ChatGPT can't answer (yet). It's a solid reminder to help you curate your content.

BE A GPS WHEN IT COMES TO CURATING YOUR CONTENT

Given the millions of pieces of content online related to your topic, your goal is not to share everything. Instead, it's best if you're like a GPS. GPS devices use mapping software to determine your location and calculate the most efficient route to your destination. It then cuts out most of the map and only shows the direct way, which helps you avoid getting lost.

When you design your sessions, your job is to do the same: Reduce their overwhelm by cutting out most of the map for your group. Curate a path that will help get them to their destination.

To be like a GPS, you need to ask:

1. Where is the group now? (Current location)

2. Where do they want to go? (Destination)

Once you can answer both those questions, you can craft your 2-Hour Workshop Mini-Mission Statement.

2-HOUR WORKSHOP MINI-MISSION STATEMENT

I prepare a simple two-sentence statement to map the workshop's purpose and objectives. Consolidating and keeping this statement sharp helps to focus your energy and decide which content to cut when designing a session.

Here's the fill-in-the-blanks template:

2-Hour Workshop Mini-Mission Statement:

This workshop is for [person] who is [currently doing and currently feeling] and wants/needs/aspires [to do this] so that [result].

The 2-Hour Workshop Mini-Mission Statement helps to identify the purpose, objectives, and results your participants desire, allowing you to tailor your workshop design accordingly.

The process of creating a mini-mission statement differs depending on the type of workshop you're hosting. There are two types:

1. Type 1: Workshops where you have access and can contact participants beforehand, or

2. Type 2: Workshops where you can't access your participants directly (for example, your workshop is part of a conference).

TYPE 1 WORKSHOP: ACCESS TO PARTICIPANTS BEFOREHAND

Here are three options for gathering information when you can contact your participants prior to your workshop.

1. Take yourself on a listening tour: Conduct interviews or surveys with participants to gather information on their challenges, aspirations, and desired outcomes.

2. Gather information using a survey.

3. Analyse the data to identify common themes and needs.

1. TAKE YOURSELF ON A LISTENING TOUR

A listening tour is another great word for 'market research' or 'informational interviews'. I like to keep these conversations brief.

The first conversation is with the person who requested your workshop. Here are some example questions you can ask during this conversation:

QUESTIONS TO ASK YOUR CLIENT

- Why did you reach out?

- How do you know this is a problem/challenge? What did you observe that brought this idea/topic to your attention?

- What are your/your team's challenges?

- How do you want the group to feel during and after this session?

- What changes would you observe in the participants if the workshop was a success?

Key logistical questions:

- How many people are attending?

- What roles are they in?

- How will they access the workshop? (Are they all attending in person, all attending online, or a mix of both?)

The feeling question:

Remember, we're designing for an experience, not just for the content, so ask this question:

- How do you want your team to feel *during* and *after* this session?

> **Tip:** Use Michael Bungay Stanier's famous "AWE" ("… and, what else?") question from his book *The Coaching Habit*, to gather more information and dig deeper. And remember, the goal is to listen, not prescribe a solution (yet).

The second conversation is with a sample of participants who are coming along to your session.

QUESTIONS FOR PARTICIPANT SAMPLE:

- What do you struggle with / what are your challenges?

- What does success in [topic] look like for you?

- What's getting in the way of your idea result right now?

- What do you need to do differently? (What's the transformation?)

- How would you know you were successful, what would that look like?

Start writing these ideas and suggestions down. If you can, avoid paraphrasing and write down what they say verbatim. If you're having these conversations virtually, ask permission if you can record them and access the call transcripts to highlight key phrases, and patterns. Some helpful AI call transcription tools include the Zoom transcribe feature (available within the Pro plan), or Otter.ai.

To keep it simple, I like to use a piece of paper, dividing it into two columns: 'Before' and 'After'.

- In the 'Before' column, I jot down the challenges and struggles the person faces.

- In the 'After' column, I write their aspirations and desired outcomes.

This exercise helps me understand how my workshop or intervention can help shift the person from their current state to their desired state. It's essential to remember that a workshop alone may not be the solution to everything, and it's necessary to be realistic about the change that can be achieved.

Current location	Destination
Capture where they are now	*Capture where they want to be*

2. GATHER INFORMATION USING A SURVEY

A pre-survey is your next best bet if you can't have a conversation. You can host a simple survey using Google Forms, Typeform, or Microsoft Forms. Try to keep your survey to three questions maximum.

If you receive a high response rate, this can also indicate the appetite for your session. But if you don't receive too many responses back, there might be a few reasons for it:

1. Maybe there's a lack of interest?

2. They're just busy (most likely, especially if you're being asked to run a Time Management session!)

3. You haven't marketed your pre-survey well/your email was lost in the hundreds of emails they received that day.

A two-hour workshop is punchy, so you don't want your pre-work to be too labour-intensive. Here's a screenshot of a survey I sent out before running a 90-minute webinar for a coaching federation last year. Note I didn't ask for names and roles or make it a requirement to respond; I only wanted to find out their motivation for attending my session.

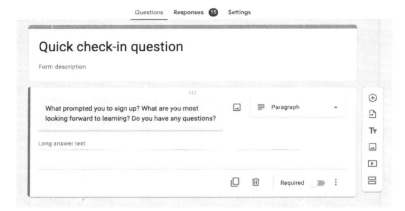

A simple survey created using Google Forms.

CASE STUDY: USING QUESTIONS TO INFORM YOUR SESSION DESIGN

Suzanne Rose is a Sergeant (Facilitator: Trainer and Assessor Support), Queensland Police Service and appeared as a guest on the *First Time Facilitator* podcast, episode 196.

She delivers facilitation skills workshop and used to assume the challenges her participants faced at work.

One day, Suzanne asked the group, "What makes a great facilitator?" and one of the participants responded saying "Someone who endeavours to understand their participants, prior to a session starting."

Suzanne she saw this as a wonderful concept to embrace.

Since then, she has emailed participants with a short, pre-workshop survey set up in Microsoft Forms.

Suzanne asks key questions to get to know her groups better, including:

- Rate your level of confidence as a facilitator of sessions/presentations in your current role. (On a 1-10 rating scale.)

- Describe any challenges or issues you have had in the past when facilitating sessions or delivering presentations. (Free text field for responses.)

- What are you hoping to get out of the workshop? (Free text field for responses.)

Knowing this upfront allows Suzanne to tailor aspects of the course based on what participants want to have addressed, switching her mindset from making assumptions to getting to know things about the participants before they step into her session. In her own words, "It's the best improvement made to the workshop in ages!"

TYPE 2 WORKSHOP: TAKE YOUR BEST GUESS

When you don't have direct access to participants beforehand, it can be challenging to identify their needs.

Here are some alternative strategies for creating a mini-mission statement. You may need to do some detective work to identify the most relevant person to approach.

At an asset management conference, I presented a session titled *"Hit the Ground Running: Creating and Sustaining Contractor Value from Day One."* Despite not being able to connect with guests, I found someone similar to them, working in a like-for-life industry. I reached out to an old friend, Vance Domin, a Maintenance Planner in Central Queensland, and asked for his input on onboarding contractors. Vance responded with his top three challenges via email, which I incorporated into a case study. The case study hit the mark.

Where else can you go for information?

Another way to take your best guess is to:

- Analyse the event description and participant list to get a sense of the audience, then research the industry or topic area to identify common needs or pain points.

- Lurk in external discussion forums or communities where your target audience/participants hang out; or linger internally, using collaboration tools like Microsoft Teams or your Slack channel, to see what challenges/opportunities/patterns emerge.

- If you're a consultant, I'd suggest seeing what conversations are occurring on sites like LinkedIn, or what articles that magazines/websites that target your participants are publishing.

Whether you have access to participants beforehand or not, there are strategies you can use to create a mini-mission statement that resonates with your group.

I'VE GOT THE DATA! NOW WHAT?

CHECKPOINT

By this stage, you should have done the following:

1. Had a conversation with your client, one or two participants, or sent out a pre-survey and captured key insights using some of the questions in this chapter.

2. Drafted a before/after profile and started to see the patterns that emerge.

3. Used this information to complete your 2-Hour Workshop Mini-Mission Statement.

Here are some examples of a mini-mission statement:

- This workshop is for agile project managers who want to optimise their use of Jira, focusing on backlog management, sprint planning, and reporting to improve their project execution and tracking.

- This workshop is for sales professionals looking to fine-tune their closing techniques to enhance their sales conversion rates.

- This workshop is for fitness trainers looking to maximise YouTube as a training platform, learning to design the perfect thumbnail, to expand their clientele and establish their personal brand.

BOB'S WORKSHOP: BEFORE AND AFTER EXAMPLE

I've captured the following:

Before (current location)	After (destination)
Feeling swamped.	Want to know what the priority is for the next 90 days.
Not sure what priorities to pursue.	Feel like they have permission to say 'no' and solely work on their priorities.
Have built up an internal customer focus and not sure how to maintain relationships by doing less; keep doing more.	Identified language and ideas to say 'no' to anything that will get in the way.

I ask Bob, *"How do you want them to feel during and after the session?"*

He replies, *"Hmm. I haven't thought about that. Well, a bit different from where we're at right now. They feel swamped and stretched, like they're pulled in all directions. I'd like them to get as much practical advice and learn how to say 'no' to other people in the business. As a team, we like maintaining relationships but not at the sacrifice of our wellbeing."*

Thanks, Bob! Now we can start drafting out the purpose of the session:

- Decide on three critical priorities for the next 90 days.

- Figure out which commitments help get there and provide the tools to build confidence to say 'no' while still maintaining business relationships.

- Share tools/systems that can help build their efficiency.

Session vibe:

- Create a calm, "I've got this" feeling in the room, empowered to push back.

I can now complete my 2-Hour Workshop Mini-Mission Statement:

This workshop is for senior leaders in the Supply Chain team who are working long hours and not feeling like they're making traction towards their department's goals. They want to refocus their energy to hit their top three targets in the next 90 days.

LEANNE, THIS IS GREAT! BUT WHERE DO I STORE MY 2-HOUR WORKSHOP MINI-MISSION STATEMENT?

I'm *so* glad you asked. Let me explain my secret weapon on the next page.

INTRODUCING: THE SPARK SHEET

Here's one of my favourite tools. It's a simple piece of paper that helps capture all your workshop details on one to two pages.

With this template, you'll be able to:

- Easily keep track of your timing and stay on schedule.

- Ensure you have the perfect mix of activities to keep your participants engaged.

- Quickly access past workshop plans and ideas for future sessions.

On the next page, you'll see what a blank SPARK Sheet looks like.

SPARK SHEET

Setup		
Workshop title: **Mini-Mission Statement:** **Session Vibe:** **Location/Time:**		**Prep:** **Pre-survey:** **Props:**
Timing	**Topic**	**Tools**
	Power Up	
	Activities	
	Review	
	Close	
Keep		

As you can see, there are three column headings: Timing, Topic and Tools (TTT):

- **Timing:** Estimate the time for each section and put the actual time in there. When you deliver your session, you can quickly tell whether you're on time, ahead, or behind.

- **Topic:** Link to your objectives and provide high-level guidance for your topic.

- **Tools:** Write the type of activity and any necessary resources, so when you pack, prepare, and set up the room, you can easily see what's required.

You can access a blank copy of the SPARK Sheet to help you with your virtual sessions at 2hourwork.shop/freebies.

You'll sleep easy knowing you have a complete SPARK Sheet for your next session. I'm old school and usually print a hard copy before all my sessions.

As we work through *The 2-Hour Workshop Blueprint*, use the SPARK Sheet, and make it your own.

HOW MUCH DETAIL SHOULD GO IN YOUR SPARK SHEET?

When I started facilitating, my workshop run sheets were pages and pages, with more in-depth timings. They were more scripted. As I'm more confident now with giving directions and I've used some of these activities before, I have less detail on my SPARK Sheet. It's up to you on what level of detail will help you feel confident and ready to rock your workshop.

CHECKPOINT

- As the GPS, describe the current location and desired destination for your workshop participants.

- Identify patterns from past conversations or feedback that could inform your workshop content.

- Reflect on a previous workshop you facilitated. How could a 2-Hour Workshop Mini-Mission Statement have improved the outcome?

CHAPTER FIVE

Curate and Cluster Your Content (Setup)

CHAPTER SUMMARY

Packaging up your content is essential to the success of your workshop. By curating your content and clustering it into three key topics, you'll be able to streamline the design process and maximise the impact of your workshop.

YOU'LL ALSO LEARN THE FOLLOWING:

- Techniques for both Subject Matter Experts and Idea Curators to source and structure content for their workshops.

- How to avoid pitfalls while researching workshop topics.

- Practical strategies for content creation and organisation.

YOU'LL WALK AWAY WITH THE FOLLOWING:

- A clear structure for your workshop, focusing on three key topics.
- The ability to create a visual framework for your workshop content.

You have a workshop mini-mission statement and a template for designing your workshop. But what will go into it? Where does this content come from?

Let's talk through the stages:

1. Dig or research.
2. Cluster into three key topics.
3. Connect your three key topics to your SPARK Sheet.

1. DIG OR RESEARCH

Dig

Digging through your own mind for workshop topics can be a great way to come up with ideas that are unique to your experience and expertise. I'd start there first, before moving to research.

Here are some tips for doing so:

- Think about the skills, knowledge, and experience that you have and how you could apply them to your workshop topic.
- Brainstorm: Make a list of all the ideas that come to mind.

Don't worry about whether they're good or not, just get them down on paper. You can refine and narrow down the list later.

- Look at trends, current events and hot topics: Consider how stories in the media can be used to help illustrate key points or provide real-world examples that can be applied to your workshop.

- Personal experience: Consider your own life experiences and how they relate to the topic of your workshop. Think about stories that illustrate key points or provide examples that can help participants understand the material better.

Research

Key tip: Before you begin your research phase, set a timer. I suggest carrying out research in 25-min sprints. Otherwise, you can spend a lot of time here. Here are some ideas/places you can go for inspiration:

- YouTube or podcasts: Create a playlist of different episodes and add them to your queue, so that when you're next out on a long drive or walk, you can research, too.

- Use reliable sources: Use reliable sources of information such as academic journals, books, and reputable websites.

- Enter your search for topics into ChatGPT. When you receive results based on case studies, or research, always ask for the source or URL, so you can fact-check it.

Will you dig or research? It depends. Workshop hosts can fall within a spectrum:

- *Subject Matter Experts (SME)*: You are highly knowledgeable in the subject area and draw from your extensive expertise to create the workshop content.

- *Idea Curators*: Your focus is on gathering and organising information from various sources to develop the workshop's material.

SMEs tend to dig, Curators tend to research (though both can and will do both!) If you'd like to discover whether you're an SME or Idea Curator, there's a questionnaire in the Helpful Extras section.

2. CLUSTER TOPICS INTO THREE KEY TOPICS

The most efficient way to organise your workshop content is to identify the three key topics, or 'umbrella topics', you'll be covering.

Identifying three key topics to focus on in your workshop can greatly simplify the design process and bring the following benefits:

1. Provides a clear structure for your workshop, making it easier to organise your content into three distinct areas.

2. Ensures that you cover all important aspects, while avoiding information overload for your participants.

3. Makes your content more memorable by breaking it down into three key elements that participants can easily recall.

LET'S JUMP IN AND FIND YOUR THREE KEY TOPICS

By the end of this activity, you'll have identified the three key focus areas for your workshop.

There are two ways to do this:

1.   Expressway

2.   Scenic route

Let's start with the expressway. If you get stuck or want another way to ideate, the scenic route is there for you, too.

Option 1: Expressway

What you need:

*   Three minutes

*   Your workshop mini-mission statement

*   A hot drink/water

*   Pen and paper

*   Timer

Instructions

1.   Prime yourself. Have your SPARK Sheet with your mini-mission statement in front of you.

2.   Now, imagine we're sitting at a cafe. I have a mocha; you've ordered a long black. The cups arrive, and you share your workshop mini-mission statement with me; I lean in and ask, "Hey, what are the three most important considerations or sub-topics *related to getting this result?*" How would you casually respond?

3.   Set your timer for three minutes. Brain-dump your ideas.

4.   After three minutes, see if there are some patterns between your ideas, and cull down to your top three topics.

5. List these three topics here:

    1._____ 2._____ and 3._____

6. Now transfer these three key ideas to your **SPARK** Sheet.

7. Then, drink a hypothetical long black. :)

Reflect

*   How did you go?

*   Easy/hard/not too sure?

*   Did you find you needed to add more topics? Is there a way that some of these sub-topics could fit under one of the above? Remember, you only have two hours!

Here's what Kim Nguyen from Core Mine said when trying this out for the first time during our 2-Hour Blueprint Masterclass: "*I had an 'aha' moment. It's interesting how you framed the question and approached it as having a conversation over a cup of coffee. I thoroughly enjoyed it. To be honest, I already had some ideas for my key topics, but putting them in a social context forced me to simplify them, making it clear and concise.*"

Here's what you just did: You stopped the torture of overthinking. I forced constraints on you by asking that question.

If you're happy with your three high-level umbrella topics, congrats!

>>> You can skip the scenic route and move on to the next chapter.

If you want an alternative approach, let's try the scenic route.

Option 2: Scenic Route

What you need:

- 30 minutes

- Your workshop mini-mission statement

- A hot drink/water

- Pen and Post-it notes

- A timer

- Oh, and most importantly, set no expectations for what's to come.

Overview

The scenic route to creating a framework for your workshop is to take some post-it notes and a timer and do a brain dump of <u>all</u> the topics related to your workshop. It's an extended version of the expressway. Then, consider your audience and what might not be necessary for them. Finally, group the remaining issues into umbrella themes.

Part One: Instructions

1. Prime yourself. Have your SPARK Sheet with your workshop mini-mission statement in front of you.

2. Set your timer for 10 minutes.

3. Brain dump everything you know about your topic with one idea per Post-it note (includes words, phrases, books, studies, videos, hacks).

4. Once the timer goes off, **step away** from the post-it notes.

5. Take a 10-min brain break, maybe go for a walk outside. Try not to play on your phone. You want to clear your head.

6. Return and set your timer for another 7 minutes.

7. Continue brainstorming one idea per post-it note.

Next, you curate your content.

Part Two: Instructions

1. Have a look and see which items are grouped. You can mind-map these ideas by moving your post-it notes and clumping together similar themes or sub-topics.

2. Now, think about your audience: Are these topics relevant to them? If not, cull. Delete. Remove. Don't tell them everything you know: Only share what they need to know.

3. Examine the remaining post-it notes: Do themes or patterns emerge?

4. Can you mind-map these and connect ideas, or have them under some key themes? Continue sorting and clumping ideas and topics; your goal is to get to three umbrella topics.

5. List these three topics here:

    1._____ 2. _____ and 3. _____

6. Now transfer these three key ideas to your SPARK Sheet.

After both the expressway and scenic route, you should have the following:

BOB'S WORKSHOP: THREE KEY IDEAS

For Bob's time management workshop, I asked myself this exact question. I didn't run to a textbook or Google "time management".

I sat with the question and wrote down a combination of these three topics:

1. **Priorities**: Being clear on what you need to do to move the needle forward for you.

2. **Discipline** and ability to say no.

3. **Systems** to cut-out some manual tasks.

CHECKPOINT:

THIS IS A CELEBRATION MOMENT

Congratulations! Once you have your three key topics, I'd love to see what you created. Please post your top three ideas on social media and tag me @leannehughes.

LEVEL UP: DISPLAY YOUR THREE KEY TOPICS USING A VISUAL

The side benefit of sharing these three key ideas is that you've created a framework. All you need to do is add a nice visual to communicate it.

For example, I might decide that all three components are important, so I'll use a Venn diagram.

Here are some examples of how you can represent your three topics visually in case you'd like to incorporate a visual into your session. I think it does help your groups retain information more, as well as communicate the relationship between your three topics.

Venn Diagram: This is a great option if all three topics are equally important to achieving the desired outcome. The overlap in the center of the diagram represents the shared qualities that all three topics possess.	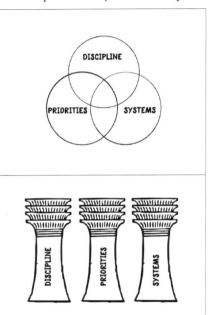
Three Pillars: Use this framework if your topics are interdependent and rely on each other to achieve the desired outcome. Each pillar represents a key topic that is essential for success.	
Three Steps: If your topics follow a sequential or prioritised order, this framework can be effective. It breaks down the process into three clear and distinct steps, each building upon the previous one.	

Pyramid: This framework is a good choice if your topics rely on each other in a hierarchical way. The base of the pyramid represents the most fundamental topic, with each level building upon the previous one.	
Make it up: Use any three objects metaphorically to represent your framework. Bonus points if it relates to the industry, or your topic. For example, I could use a clock to represent time management.	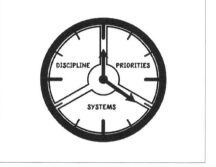

If you choose to visually represent your model, you can use tools like SmartArt within Microsoft Office to design it, or Canva.

3. CONNECT YOUR THREE KEY TOPICS TO YOUR SPARK SHEET

Now that you have your three key topics, let's see how they drive your design. As you can see, I have estimated my rough timings, and now I've thrown my three topics under the Activities section.

Setup		
Workshop title:	**Prep:**	
Mini-Mission Statement: *This workshop is for senior leaders in the Supply Chain team who are working long hours and not feeling like they're making traction towards their department's goals. They want to refocus their energy to hit their top three targets in the next 90 days.*	**Pre-survey:** **Props**	
Session Vibe:		
Location/Time:		

Timing	Topic	Tools
08:30	**Power Up**	
09:00		
09:20	**Activities** Topic One: Priorities	
09:45	Topic Two: Discipline	
10:10	Topic Three: Systems	
10:35	**Review**	
11:00	Close	
Keep		

Great! It's starting to take shape.

INTERMISSION

INTERMISSION: BUILD THE BUZZ: GET YOUR GROUPS SHOWING UP READY, INVESTED, AND ACTIVE

Let's get tactical and dive into how I invest in the success of the workshops I deliver. This is a critical phase that comes after the Setup and before your actual session, typically around one to two weeks before. It's a golden opportunity to build trust and set expectations with your participants.

To increase bookings and the attendance rate, here are three strategies to consider:

1. Don't wait to communicate: Start generating hype and excitement early on.

2. Craft an attractive workshop title that grabs attention and piques curiosity.

3. Implement an array of preventative tactics to encourage people to show up.

DON'T WAIT TO COMMUNICATE

The best way to get skin in the game is to start communicating with your group before your session. I usually set up a workshop one-page site on my own website, or a Notion page which includes:

- Pre-workshop video (1-2 minutes): Pique the participants' curiosity and interest about the session, and the host (you!).

- A quick check-in question.

- Sharing key logistical information, like what to bring, and what time to arrive.

Pre-workshop video

Create a pre-event video to build anticipation and excitement. Use a simple 60-120-second video to introduce the topic and yourself, give a preview of what to expect, and leave a few surprises. You can create a video survey using VideoAsk, Loom, or upload your video to YouTube as an unlisted video.

Quick check-in question

Use a pre-event check-in to build excitement. This is a different survey that serves a secondary purpose – to build the buzz. Start with a simple yes/no question, followed by a brief open-ended question, asking participants a question like, "What are you most excited to learn?"

Sharing key logistical information

Include details like date, time and what to bring, plus:

- In-person event: Where to park, who to see when they arrive, dress code.

- Virtual event: Resend the video conferencing details and include a time-zone converter

EXAMPLE

TECHNOLOGY:

- I recorded this video using QuickTime on my Mac. You can also record it using your phone.

- AI captions made by Descript.

- This video was uploaded to YouTube as an unlisted video, and I embedded the link in Notion.

- The Google Forms survey was also in Notion, underneath the video, so I only needed to share one link, a Notion page. Following the session, the same Notion page turned into the hub for all course resources.

Grab an editable script template for your introductory video and Notion templates at 2hourwork.shop/freebies.

SCRIPT:

"Thank you so much for jumping in and signing up for the *Group Coaching Masterclass* that kicks off next Friday.

Remember, if you're in America it's Thursday evening, and you should have the calendar details. If not, please shoot me an email.

This is a video to say, hello, and I'd also like you to have a think about this: *What do you think is the application of a group coaching program? I want you to consider, how could you leverage it? How could you add it to something that you offer already?* Or if you don't currently do that, *Where are the opportunities for you to add it to your suite of offerings?"*

That's a question we'll dive into when we jump into the call next week. So how the format works is that the Friday session is two hours. That is the masterclass. This is where a lot of the content will be explored. It's still interactive. Then, you have a bit of a break before we jump in the following Wednesday for the encore round. The encore is in a Question-and-Answer format. All recordings are available on the private podcast, so you can listen in, anytime!

All resources are on this website where you're viewing this video. All resources, documents, templates, and links will be available here, too. Bookmark it now!

That's it for me. I look forward to meeting all of you. If there's anything else in your mind, please complete the quick question below and that might help me target this even better for you for next Friday.

Chat to you soon!

Here's another example of a site I created for a 90-minute webinar for a global humanitarian organisation.

WHAT TO EXPECT: COURAGEOUS CONVERSATIONS IN A GLOBAL WORKPLACE: **CREATING A GLOBAL COMMUNITY OF TRUST & BELONGING FACILITATED BY: LEANNE HUGHES**

STEP 1: WATCH THE 90 SECOND VIDEO BELOW.

STEP 2: TEST YOUR TECH BEFORE THE CALL

This will be an interactive workshop, so I'd love us to be able to hear and see each other. You can test out your technology at this site: **https://zoom.us/test**

STEP 3: REFLECT ON THIS QUESTION:

Think about a time, an event, a scenario where you felt like you really belonged. You felt like you could contribute, and be yourself. What 1 or 2 things transpired for you to feel that way?

OPTIONAL EXTRA STEP:

If you have any questions related to this topic, challenges or opportunities you'd like me to discuss on the call, please submit it using the form below.

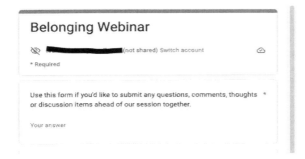

CRAFT AN ATTRACTIVE WORKSHOP TITLE THAT GRABS ATTENTION AND PIQUES CURIOSITY

When I was the marketing manager for a large training organisation, we renamed our *Effective Email Management* course to *Email Hell to Email Heaven* and saw a surge in registrations. This is the power of a captivating title and I believe it's worth investing attention into getting it right.

Here are some ideas on how you can come up with a winning workshop title:

Idea	Example
Go for the transformation: Use "From [X] to [Y]."	*From Reactive to Proactive: A Time Management Workshop for Supply Chain Leaders*
Define the result: Too often, we name a workshop based on the methodology. What results does your workshop bring?	*Time for Change: Transforming Supply Chain Productivity*
Focus on the outcome: Create a title that emphasises the benefits or outcomes that participants will get from your workshop.	*Powered-Up Productivity: A Time Management Workshop for Busy Supply Chain Leaders*
Use your audience's language: Find words that your target audience is using.	I once advertised a webinar about *Creating engaging workshop experiences*, then I noticed someone posted in my group about avoiding non-boring sessions. I changed my webinar title to, *Creating non-boring workshop experiences* and registrations exploded!

Make it catchy: Use puns, humour, or alliteration (my favourite!) to make your title memorable and appealing.	*Efficient Ever After: Time Management Strategies for Supply Chain Excellence*
Keep it short and simple: Avoid confusing people with complex words or phrases. Keep the title short, simple, and easy to understand.	*Master Your Schedule*
Embrace clickbait: Add curiosity and mix it with a listicle: My friend Joeri Schilders and I ran a webinar called *5 ways to ramp up the energy in your workshops (by being a bit lazy).*	*5 Surprising Time Management Techniques for Supply Chain Leaders*
Be relevant: Is there a way to weave in current trends, events, or pop culture to your workshop's topic to your session?	*Get More Done in Less Time: What Supply Chain Leaders can Learn from Tim Ferriss*

IMPLEMENT AN ARRAY OF PREVENTATIVE TACTICS TO ENCOURAGE PEOPLE TO SHOW UP

To boost your session's show-up rate, here are some tactics to prevent drop-outs you might like to consider.

- **Timing:** Assess the timing of your workshop: Generally, morning sessions tend to have better attendance rates compared to afternoon or evening sessions.

- **Influence:** Consider who sends out the initial communication: If your workshop is an internal one, consider having a senior leader send out the invitation. This can result in a better response rate, compared to if it's sent out by the training team.

- **Quick yes/no email**: Send a personalised email a week prior to the workshop, asking for a simple yes/no response. (See example below).

- **Calendar commute**: Send a separate invite for *commute time*: If your workshop starts at 9am, send a separate invite for 15 minutes prior as 'commute time', even if the session is virtual.

- **Set up chat groups**: If your workshop group has more than 10 participants, create mini-hubs or chat groups through tools like WhatsApp or Microsoft Teams to foster a sense of community and connection.

- **'Invite' > 'Request'**: Use the term 'invitation' instead of 'meeting request'. An invitation implies a personal invitation from the organiser, which can make the recipient feel valued and appreciated. This subtle shift in language can encourage greater participation and engagement from participants.

QUICK YES/NO EMAIL EXAMPLE

I was in Brisbane, flying to Singapore the following week to attend a Psychotactics workshop.

An email landed in my inbox from Renuka at Psychotactics.

Subject line: Quick Question

Email body: Hi Leanne, Renuka here from Psychotactics. Quick question. Have you bought The Brain Audit and read it? R.

I replied immediately with a "No" because it was an easy question to answer.

What I liked about this email was that it was personalised and straightforward, making me feel accountable to respond.

If you need people to pre-read or watch a specific video before your workshop, try this strategy. Instead of sending an email to the entire group, craft a two-sentence email for everyone.

When I asked Renuka about this strategy, she shared that she could predict who would attend the workshop (or not), based on how quickly they responded, or if they responded at all.

SPARK SHEET UPDATE

My setup session is complete. I've added in details including the workshop title, session vibe, prep, pre-survey, and props (what to bring).

Setup	
Workshop title: We've got this: Refocus for the next 90 days. **Mini-mission statement:** This workshop is for senior leaders in the Supply Chain team who are working long hours and not feeling like they're making traction towards their department's goals. They want to refocus their energy to hit their top three targets in the next 90 days. **Session vibe:** Create a calm, "I've got this" feeling in the room. **Location/Time:** The Awesome Room, 9 am start (room booked for 8 am).	**Prep:** Pre-video announcing two things: pre-Survey and what to bring **Pre-survey:** What's getting in the way of you achieving your Q1 priorities? **Props:** Work calendar (digital or paper planner is fine)

CHECKPOINT

1. Think about one logistical detail you've overlooked in past workshops. How can you communicate this detail more effectively in future?

2. Reflect on the example of renaming the *Effective Email*

Management course. How can a creative title make a difference in your own workshop?

3.   Write a draft title for your next workshop and share it with a colleague or friend. Ask for feedback and revise it based on their suggestions.

I hope you enjoyed the intermission. Let's move on to Act II.

ACT

II

Across the next three chapters, you'll explore
questions, ideas and activities to bring your
workshop to life. You'll add detail to your SPARK
Sheet, outlining what's involved in your pre-start,
your opening, and the bulk of your workshop.

CHAPTER SIX

P is for Power Up

CHAPTER SUMMARY

The Power Up section is an opportunity to connect with your participants and set the tone for the session. Use this time to establish trust, create a sense of safety, and build excitement for the topic.

YOU'LL LEARN THE FOLLOWING:

- The benefits of starting your workshop early, even before it officially begins.

- How to prepare yourself both backstage and on stage to encourage immediate participation from your participants.

- The value of asking low-friction questions to kick off your session, and where to find inspiration for them.

YOU'LL WALK AWAY WITH THE FOLLOWING:

- A completed Power Up section for your SPARK Sheet.

- Three shiny new ways to start your workshop.

Starting your workshop well is crucial (no pressure!). Let's spin the focus to kicking off your session.

DO:

- Set expectations.

- Provide key logistical details.

- Establish trust and create a welcoming environment.

- Begin the session with energy and focus.

- Clearly articulate the problem or challenge and the benefits it will provide.

- Address and overcome potential objections or concerns before they arise.

- Encourage participants to reflect on their current situation to increase investment.

DON'T:

- Ignore your group before your session starts.

- Start your session with housekeeping ("Hi, the toilets are located here" has never won anyone over in the first two minutes).

- Start your session by telling your life story.

P STANDS FOR POWER UP

There are two parts:

1. **Personal power-up:** Fine-tune your backstage process so that you can approach the workshop with a confident and relaxed demeanour, setting a positive tone for your group.

2. **Power up your participants**: Energise your group before the start of a session.

THE DAY BEFORE (PERSONAL POWER-UP)

The most significant predictor of how your group will show up is how you show up. If you appear nervous or stressed, your group can feel that, too. When you see a workshop host or speaker pacing around the room, constantly adjusting their PowerPoint slides, it doesn't give a sense of confidence, right? Getting your backstage process finessed is vital because you can relax and switch your focus to engaging when people arrive once you're done.

Without stating the obvious, **getting a good night's sleep** makes the biggest difference. I have run sessions off only a couple of hours of sleep because of time zones and because I was stressing about the session and wondering how I would go. Everything was so much more complicated!

Once you tackle the first 15 minutes with confidence, the rest will flow smoothly

Having a sense of completeness helps me sleep better. Here are some ways I prepare that you might find helpful:

- Print out and complete your SPARK Sheet beforehand to avoid last-minute rushing.

- Decide on your outfit and have it ironed and ready to go.

- Practice delivering the first 15 minutes of your session, so you feel confident and prepared. Getting this part out of the way can help set the tone for the rest of the session.

- Pack all the necessary items and have a checklist ready to refer to when you arrive at the venue or virtual room. (I love a checklist so that I don't wake up in the middle of the night thinking, "Did I pack my clicker?" You can document everything you need to bring in your SPARK Sheet. This is where the Tools section is convenient. If I'm sharing resources like websites, iPad screen, sound or video, or a flipchart in the background, it's documented to help me avoid any last-minute scrambling).

These tips can help you feel more organised and prepared, allowing you to focus on delivering an engaging workshop.

Here's my workshop packing list for an in-person session. You can grab this template and personalise it for you: Visit

2hourwork.shop/freebies.

Me		
☐ Business cards	☐ Hand sanitiser	☐ Snacks (fruit, nuts)
☐ Drink-bottle	☐ Panadol	☐ Soothers
☐ Eye drops	☐ Pen	☐ Tissues
☐ Green tea bag		

Office Supplies		
☐ A4 clear protector/ display sheets	☐ Dependable stapler and staples	☐ Post-it notes
☐ Art of Conversation cards	☐ Dot stickers - need to vote, prioritise ideas	☐ Printout of slide handouts
☐ Attendance sheet	☐ Feedback sheets	☐ Props (ensure they add value)
☐ Ballpoint pens	☐ Flipchart	☐ Scissors
☐ Blu-tac	☐ Flipchart pens - Mr Sketch or Neuland	☐ Sticky tape
☐ Course materials/ resources/ workbook - (course dependent)	☐ Flipchart stand	☐ Tennis balls x 3
	☐ Mints for table / and bowls to store these	☐ Tibetan bell
		☐ Tent cards/ name badges
		☐ Whiteboard markers and duster

Technology		
☐ Any resources like videos or presentations or handouts also saved onto the USB	☐ Computer cables with multiple inputs for HDMI, VGA, and USB all in one	☐ Speakers - Bluetooth/ AUX
		☐ Phone
☐ Batteries for clicker	☐ Laptop	☐ Phone charger
☐ Clicker	☐ Laptop charger	☐ Presentation - on laptop, + saved on a USB

ON THE DAY (PERSONAL POWER-UP)

It's also essential for you to get into state. "State" refers to your emotional and mental condition at any given time. It's how you feel and what's going on in your head. For example, you could be in a calm state, an anxious state, or an energised state. Even though I've delivered hundreds of workshops, I honestly still feel a sense of trepidation, even though I try to be playful. So, to work on my state, I have a pre-workshop ritual. As you spend more time delivering sessions, find out what works best for you.

Warm yourself up: Develop your pre-workshop ritual

Here are samples of the activities that help me get into state:

- Exercise in the morning to get rid of any nerves or jitters of excitement, preferably an outdoor run.

- Journal any self-doubts. One time I wrote, "No matter how this session goes, my dogs still love me." It made me laugh but also put things into perspective.

- I'll play my Get In State Spotify playlist on the drive-in featuring songs like "Don't You Worry" by Swedish House Mafia, and "Scream & Shout" by will.i.am and Britney Spears. Curate your playlist. Find what songs inspire you and make you feel good.

- Stretch and warm up my voice. Look at Julian Treasure's TED talk, "How to speak so that people want to listen" – the exercises around the six-minute mark are short, sharp, and effective.

- Keep the group front of mind and ask, "How can I serve this group the best way today?" (It's always helpful to switch the focus onto your group. When I interviewed keynote speaker Neen James, she shared this quote, "If you stand in service, you won't be nervous.")

In the room

- Arrive early and be prepared to move furniture around: I was hosting a CliftonStrengths session for a leadership team only recently. I spent the first twenty minutes lugging around chairs, that's why it's great to arrive an hour early.

- Be tech-ready: The last thing you want when people arrive is to fiddle around with PowerPoint and technology and be a sweaty mess. By the way, always plan for your tech to fail. That's why I often plan to not use technology for in-person sessions. If you're using PowerPoint or another tool, have the file open on your laptop, so you can easily test it.

- Write your name, the workshop topic and the venue's wi-fi password on a flipchart/whiteboard up the front of the room. If you're closing the door, maybe ensure your workshop topic is on the door, so that someone arriving late knows they're walking into the right place.

- Have another piece of flipchart paper handy, or whiteboard space available for your workshop's Parking Lot. The Parking Lot is a term used to describe topics, questions, or issues that come up during a workshop but are not addressed in full due to time constraints or other reasons. These items are often recorded and saved for future reference.

- Make sure the room is set up and ready to go.

IN THE VIRTUAL ROOM

Here's my checklist for virtual workshop preparation. You can grab a free editable copy at 2hourwork.shop/freebies.

Workshop intention

☐ Read your workshop mini-mission statement.

Personal presentation

☐ Double-check your calendar to confirm time (I usually book out 30 mins before any "big" live calls in my calendar, too, so that I don't feel so rushed)

☐ Glass of water (and a jug to top up)

☐ Check your background

☐ Notepad and pen handy

☐ Check second / backup device (for example, mobile phone personal hotspot in case your internet

☐ Ensure you can see the time easily

☐ Write any reminders/prompts on post-it notes and stick on computer monitor

☐ Warm up your voice

☐ Breathe, relax, smile

Family/housemate tips

☐ Hang a *Do Not Disturb* sign on your door / advise how long you'll be on your call

☐ If it's a critical meeting, ask them to hop off Netflix/ streaming, so it doesn't chew your data

Tech preparation

☐ Frame up your camera

☐ Switch lighting on

☐ Test your sound

☐ Put your phone on silent / Focus mode

☐ Close any tabs and applications you don't need

☐ If you're sharing slides, or websites, have these open in advance

☐ Add any important tech instructions / directions for your participants into a Notes file, so that you can easily paste these into Chat

☐ Turn notifications off on your computer and log out of any messaging apps (for example, Microsoft Teams)

☐ Hop onto your call 10-15 mins early to check your background, lighting and sound

Now that you're prepared and ready to go, let's switch the focus to what's happening in your workshop room.

JUMP THE GUN: START YOUR WORKSHOP BEFORE IT OFFICIALLY BEGINS (PARTICIPANT POWER-UP)

I've never missed a flight. If I had to create corporate values for myself, the number one value would be *punctuality*.

So, you can imagine my delighted surprise when I, as a participant, arrived at a workshop 20 minutes early, only to find that things were already in full swing. This happened during Dr. Cathryn Lloyd and Andrew Rixon's book launch/seminar of "The Story Cookbook" in Brisbane. When I walked in, there were flipcharts with thought-provoking questions on the wall (like, "What does community-building mean to you?), light music playing, and a lot of chatter among participants.

It was much better than arriving in silence, taking a seat, and browsing my phone. We were already warmed up and eager to participate when the session officially started. Starting the session with activities, discussions, and energy already creates a more engaging and dynamic workshop experience.

P stands for Power Up. This includes creating interaction and getting people in the right mindset for the workshop before it begins. It can be as simple as having a whiteboard with prompts for people to write on or creating involvement early by getting them to do something. The key is to create an inviting and engaging atmosphere as soon as people arrive. And remember, you can always play music to set the mood too!

What's great about a pre-start is that it helps to transition people from where they were before your workshop to being totally present at your session. You want to signal that they're in a different space. It creates a fundamental change, a mood shift, helping them feel a sense of ease before your workshop officially starts.

At the Intermission, we explored what you can do a week or two before your session starts. Now, let's get ready to launch.

FIFTEEN MINUTES BEFORE YOUR SESSION STARTS (PARTICIPANT POWER-UP)

Here are some suggestions to create that warmth in your sessions beforehand. Pick one or two of these techniques; you don't need to do all of them:

- Engage with participants individually by welcoming them and asking them how their morning has been. Also, sense if someone wants to engage or not. Sometimes someone has dropped in early and wants to pick their seat and continue emailing or doing their work. That's fine, too! No need to infringe on their space; it's just opening it up as an opportunity.

- Provide a quick question to get the conversation started. You can have this on a slide or a flipchart. Relate it to your topic, like, *"What's your 1 tip for managing your time?"*, *"What's more important to manage, time or energy?"* These questions prime your group (another P word!).

- Have a tea/coffee station to allow participants to gather and relax.

- Provide an engaging activity: Offer participants a task to complete as they arrive, such as filling in a name card or a tent card on their table, or assigning them a role, like directing others to the refreshments area. Here are a couple of excellent suggestions from The Flipchart community on Facebook (feel free to join us!):

  - Felicity Neeson uses laminated sheets with rebus puzzles (a rebus is a picture representation of a name, work, or phrase). The sheets are laminated, allowing participants to respond using whiteboard markers, and easily wiped clean afterward.

  - Rachel Ozazki recommends offering other fun, simple activities, such as a 100-piece puzzle for participants to work on, colouring sheets, themed crosswords, beginner-friendly Sudoku, origami, brain teasers, ink blot interpretation (what do you see?), sensory fidgets, and Lego™.

BOB'S WORKSHOP: PRE-START EXAMPLE

I'll write a thought-provoking question on a piece of flipchart paper: *"What's more important to manage: energy or time?"* if nothing else, it can start a conversation or prime the group for your topic.

JUMPING THE GUN: VIRTUAL SESSION

Here are some ideas to enhance your virtual workshops:

- Include a note in the meeting invitation, informing participants that you'll be online 10-15 minutes early for anyone who'd like to test their technology.

- Customise your Zoom waiting room with a welcoming message. You can do this in the Zoom settings.

- Open the meeting room early and have your video on, if someone arrives, start engaging them in conversation, so that when the next person comes, they think, "Oh, I better start talking and contributing!" as opposed to everyone jumping into your session with cameras off – that's contagious, too.

- When admitting someone from the waiting room, greet them with a smile or wave to make them feel welcome.

- Invite a respected member of the group to join early and set the tone for participation. This is a ninja move. People often look to others for cues on how to behave, so seeing an influential person engaging can inspire others to do the same.

- Join the call early with a coffee mug in hand, signaling that you're open for conversation.

- Post a question in Chat to initiate discussion and promote engagement. As more people join, continue sharing the question to warm up the conversation. Leading with energy and encouraging involvement from the start sets a positive tone. For example, you could ask, "Welcome! It's great to have you here. As you join, feel free to unmute or share in the chat: What are you excited to learn about today?"

REDUCE THE FRICTION

One way to increase engagement during a workshop is to reduce friction and make it easy for participants to answer questions and get involved from the start. Providing multiple options can make it easier for everyone to get involved. Some people prefer to speak up during a group discussion, while others like to write down their thoughts or share in a smaller breakout group.

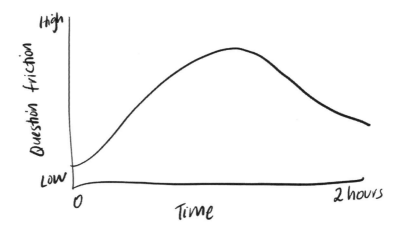

Friction question: High and low vs. workshop time

Your goal at the start is to ask low-friction questions to start building involvement. Low-friction questions require minimal effort on the participant's part to answer.

For example:

- What one word comes to mind when you think about teamwork?

- Any "Would you rather" questions (or a closed question).

- A game of overrated/underrated (throw up some statements/words and ask people to share, whether they think it's overrated or underrated. For example: "Is kale overrated or underrated?")

What you might notice about these questions is that they're simple to answer. They don't require a substantial cognitive load. When finding good questions that boost engagement in workshops, one great place to start is online communities such as Facebook Groups and Pinterest boards. These platforms are a wealth of information and inspiration for all things related to workshop design and facilitation.

HERE ARE SOME FUN PRE-START QUESTIONS

- What's your favourite 3 pm snack of choice? (Thanks again, Steph Clarke. Great question!)

- What are you currently reading or watching?

- What's something you're excited about or looking forward to? (Prompts a more positive vibe.)

A website that I recommend for these types of questions is https://icebreaker.range.co/.

At the start of your workshop, **avoid high-friction** questions like:

- "If you were CEO tomorrow, what changes would you make?"

- "Why do you do what you do?"

- "What's the meaning of life?"

You get my drift. Hard to answer.

EVEN DRINKING GAMES CAN INSPIRE YOUR LOW-FRICTION ACTIVITIES

My best (non-professional) suggestion is to find a drinking game that you can tailor towards your topic. I know that sounds a bit crazy but think about it: Drinking games are all about low friction:

- They require little instruction

- Are easy to play

- Make people laugh (even without alcohol)

One of my favourite games is *The 5 Second Game*. It's a board game that's quick and warms up your brain and voice. Perfect for a two-hour workshop!

NEVER START A WORKSHOP WITH HOUSEKEEPING

"Hi, my name is Leanne Hughes. There is coffee and tea at the back, the fire exits are to the left, and the toilets are just outside the door to the right."

If you start a workshop explaining where the fire exits and toilets are, you're doing it wrong.

We're not travelling on an aircraft that's about to take off. You have time to talk logistics. In my podcast, *First Time Facilitator*, I share that the goal is to create an unpredictable workshop experience that predictably works. To do that and gain attention, it helps to break the mould.

Here's a high-level overview of how I usually start a session.

- **Introduction:**
  - o Welcome.
  - o Quick story related to the topic.
  - o Overview of the session.
  - o Personal introduction (keep it short, 90 seconds max).
  - o Objections/Scope clarification.
- **Logistics:**
  - o Cover key details you need from a compliance perspective (fire exits, bathroom) and introduce the Parking Lot (any topics, questions, or issues that come up during a workshop but are not addressed in full due to time constraints or other reasons).
  - o Online session details (set the standard for how to participate, like how to engage in Chat, use the reactions, raise your hand to come off-mute).
- **Buckle-up approach**
  - o Help connect participants to the content using either the *Deep-end, Three-question sequence* or *Playback approach.*

BUCKLE-UP APPROACH

The buckle-up approach is a way to introduce your key topics to your group upfront and help them connect to the content.

Let's demonstrate this with Bob's workshop example:

> **BOB'S WORKSHOP: BUCKLE-UP EXAMPLE**
>
> Here's how I'd explain the instruction:
>
> "Managing priorities is a huge topic! For today's session, I'd like us to focus on three key priority areas (excuse the pun). You should grab a piece of paper and draw three columns. On the first column, I'd like you to write the word *Priorities*; on the second column, I'd like you to write the word *Discipline;* and on the third column, I'd like you to write the word *Systems*.

Give yourself a rating from 1-5 for each of these; where 1 is "I'm not strong at this" to 5 which is "I love this, it's my strength!" I'd like you to consider how you run your workday, week, and month.

- In the **Priorities** column: How clear are you on your priorities? If I was to ask you to list the top three work priorities, could you do that easily? If so, give yourself a 5. If you have no idea, a 1. If you're somewhere in between, give yourself that rating.

- Let's move to **Discipline**: At work, we have to build relationships all the time, and sometimes, we might relate that to people-pleasing: Accepting all meetings even though we don't know why we're being invited, taking a lot on, doing work for others that might be outside your scope (that's a 1). On the other hand, we may be good at guarding our time, pushing back, saying 'no' to meetings where we're not sure, and being mindful of where our energy and time go and protecting it. If so, give yourself a 5.

- Finally, we have **Systems**. There are so many ways to manage your time! How cleverly are you using your tools, and not only technology, like planners, calendars, or lists? Do you know what works for you and is working for you right now? If so, give yourself a 5. If you feel you could use some help in this area, if you feel like you could improve a lot in this area, give yourself a 1.

Thank you. What I'd like you to do now is turn to the person next to you or get into groups of three.

You don't need to share your numbers, but I'd like you to have a conversation based on your self-ratings:

- Which column for you had the highest rating? Priority, Discipline, or Systems? Why is that?

- Which column would you like to focus on and improve? Why is that?

- Before I get you back together as a group. I'd like you to identify a spokesperson/someone in your group who can share one high-level key theme from your group conversation.

- You'll each have a minute to share. Are there any questions? Off you go."

Following these instructions, I'll give the groups 5-7 minutes to discuss, call them back, and ask for a share back.

The great thing about the buckle-up approach is that the data or number doesn't really matter; it's the reason why they give themselves the number that drives the conversation.

Use it as a self-assessment at the beginning of your workshop to get a baseline measure, PLUS you can revisit it at the end of your workshop as a reflection piece. What's not to love?!

BUCKLE-UP INSTRUCTIONS: A BREAKDOWN

- Restate the objective: For today's session, we will look at the mix of these three ingredients to help you [get the result you're after].

- What they did: You self-assessed where you were against this model.

- Instructions: In a moment... ("In a moment" is a crucial phrase. If you miss it, people start looking around for who they can work with. "In a moment" gives them time to absorb your instructions. Thank you to Nikki McMurray for sharing that with me!) ...what I'd like you to do is turn to the person next to you, or get into groups of three. You don't need to share your numbers, but I'd like you to have a conversation and share the following:

  o Which column for you had the highest rating? [Insert your three things]
    - Why is that?
  o Which column for you allows you to grow the most?
    - Why is that?

- Tell them what I want to get and their output. Ask for a group spokesperson, as you're still building trust. *I'd like you to identify a spokesperson/someone in your group who can share one high-level key theme from your group conversation.*

> It is a nice specific ask, rather than asking them to share their entire conversation.
>
> - You'll each have a minute to share (Give them specifics on what they need to do).
>
> - Are there any questions? Checking in to see if they understand.
>
> - Off you go (a nice Australian way of saying "Over to you!")

The breakdown here works for any instruction.

Specificity in your instructions is critical. For example, instead of asking a broad question like, "What are some ways we can improve performance?", try asking "What are **two ways** we can increase performance?" This is even more important in a virtual workshop before you send people out to breakout groups.

The buckle-up approach is my favourite way to begin because you're teaching the framework while helping people understand it by connecting it to their own lives. It grabs attention immediately because people expect you to start sharing information but instead, you're asking them to reflect on their own lives. This ramps up the relevance of your topic.

If you'd prefer other ways to start, here are some alternatives:

1. Playback method

2. Deep end approach

3. Three-question sequence

1. PLAYBACK METHOD

If you sent out a pre-session survey (part of your Setup), now is a good time to playback those themes and share the results/patterns identified. I tend to try to find 3-4 underlying patterns of responses that I share that with the group. I turn to them and ask, "*Out of these four phrases, which one resonates with you most today? Turn to the person next to you and have a conversation.*"

The advantage of this approach is that you're using their language (don't paraphrase what you get, it's best if you keep it as it is). This helps make them feel like they belong and that the session is relevant to them. It also allows them to share any additional thoughts or ideas that didn't come up in the survey responses. Following that paired response, I invited some groups to share their discussion.

Here's an example of the responses I received to a survey about delivering virtual workshops. I delivered this session on Zoom and shared this slide, using the 3-2-1 game to gather feedback.

3-2-1 INSTRUCTIONS EXAMPLE

Open Chat and enter the option (1, 2, 3 or 4) that you resonate with the most.

Wait for my signal and countdown before hitting Enter.

What's your biggest challenge?

1. Engagement, lack of feedback, not able to see and connect with people.
2. The technology might fail on me!
3. Making sure people feel comfortable and can contribute.
4. Keeping it interesting and getting my presentation materials right.

In the 3-2-1 game, I get people to enter the option that resonates with them most into the Chat box but ask them not to click Enter. Then I countdown ("3-2-1- GO!"), and you see the Chat box light up with responses. I love to do this at the beginning of a session, as the Chat box usually blows up and sets a tone for instant engagement. Thanks to my Virtually Possible collaborator, Joeri Schilders for this tactic.

2. THE DEEP END APPROACH

The deep end approach is about jumping in immediately, asking your groups to respond to a scenario without providing any upfront content or information. I love this approach and find it quite refreshing, as you assume your group members all have experience or ideas, and even if not, it's an excellent way to identify where they are and how they think about your topic.

I create a scenario that relates to their work and buckles them into the topic.

BOB'S WORKSHOP: DEEP END EXAMPLE

Scenario:

"You've been offered the most incredible opportunity at work! But you realise it will take up an extra six hours each week for the next three months. It's a no-brainer; you must take this project on. However, you're already maxed out your calendar."

What do you do? How do you free up your time to take on this 'pinch me' project?"

I ask them to individually reflect on this question, and then get into groups to discuss the response. I'll ask each group to share their top three ideas.

The big question I ask after the debrief is, *"These are all great ideas. What's stopping you from gaining these six hours back right now?"*

Following this, I'd share the Venn diagram, explain the elements, connect their responses, and kick-off.

The deep end approach is great for getting your workshop participants buckled in from the start.

3. THE THREE-QUESTION SEQUENCE

Using a reliable three-question sequence can effectively engage people in a workshop. Here's how it works:

- Question One is a low-friction question to get them talking (warm-up question).

- Question Two gets them connected to the topic (focus question).

- Question Three is the question you want to debrief as a group. It's the one that gets to the heart of what people want to learn about in the workshop (bingo question).

Here are some examples of a three-question sequence I might use in a leadership session:

- Question 1 (warm-up question): *"Would you rather be bored or busy?"* This is an easy question for people to answer (there are only two options!) and gets them involved immediately. Search for "Would you rather" online; there are some great ones available.

- Question 2 (focus question): *"Think about someone great you worked for; what one thing stood out for you about the way they lead their team?"*

- Question 3 (bingo question): *"What do you think are the biggest challenges leaders currently face, or will face?"* or *"What's one thing you want to learn today?"*

This three-question sequence is a flexible tool that can quickly adapt to different topics and audiences. The sequencing matters. Start with your 'easiest to answer' question first and work your way in to connect to your case.

Now that you've glanced through various options, start crafting your SPARK Sheet.

BOB'S WORKSHOP: UPDATED SPARK SHEET

Timing	Topic	Tools
08:30	**Power Up** Have the following ready 30 mins before the session starts: • Flipchart stand, pre-prepared flipchart and pens • Post-its and highlighters on table	Write question on flipchart

09:00	• **Introduction:**
	   o Welcome
	   o Calendar Tetris story:
	   o Overview of the session: Ask Bob why he requested this session
	   o Personal introduction (keep it short, 90 seconds max)
	   o Objections/Scope clarification
	• **Logistics:**
	   o Ask questions anytime!
	   o Housekeeping not required
	• **Buckle-up approach**
	   o Priorities
	   o Discipline
	   o Systems
	• **Strongest/Improve?** Individually reflect and share back
		• Flipchart + pen to draw Venn diagram
		• Paired discussion

09:20	**Activities** Topic One: Priorities	
09:45	Topic Two: Discipline	
10:10	Topic Three: Systems	
10:35	**Review**	
11:00	Close	

CHECKPOINT

- Consider your pre-workshop rituals. Do they help you to get in the right state of mind? If not, what changes could you make?

- How do you currently set up your physical or virtual workshop space? How might changes in this area affect the workshop's success?

- Reflect on the type of questions you ask at the start of a workshop. Are they low-friction and easy to answer, or do they require more cognitive effort?

CHAPTER SEVEN

A is for Activities

CHAPTER SUMMARY

The bulk of the time in your session is spent in the Activities section. This is where your content comes to life through activity and discussion.

YOU'LL LEARN THE FOLLOWING:

- The key ingredient for keeping energy and involvement through your session.

- The perfect amount of time to balance your talking with their involvement.

- How to deal with unknowns during your session.

YOU'LL WALK AWAY WITH THE FOLLOWING:

- A variety of activities you can use to bring your SPARK Sheet to life.

- A completed Activities section in your SPARK Sheet.

In the Activities section, you will share information, facilitate discussions, and lead exercises that energise and engage participants. The section's purpose is to use various activities to change the atmosphere, prompt discussions, and encourage participation.

DO:

- Use various formats and techniques to keep participants engaged.

- Align content with the workshop's specific goals and objectives.

- Incorporate interactive elements and hands-on learning opportunities.

- Continuously evaluate and adjust content to ensure relevance and value for the group.

DON'T:

- Deliver a lecture.

- Wait till the end of your session to answer questions.

- Hold to your agenda so tightly that there is no room for conversation or interaction.

TIMING

The Activities section is the bulk of your workshop, approximately 70-75 minutes. The secret to keeping your group interested is to mix it up.

You'll be sharing ideas on three different topics for approximately 25 minutes. Each 25-minute chunk consists of context-setting, application, and discussion.

WEAVING IN CONTRAST THROUGH YOUR WORKSHOP DESIGN

Weaving in contrast is like hearing a key change in a song. You may get a bit sick of the repetitive chorus, but once you hear a key change, the mood and energy shift. That's what you're creating in a workshop when you introduce contrast. A good key change reinvigorates your group.

Let's draw this analogy back to our workshops. The key is to continue changing things up in your SPARK Sheet. This may sound difficult, but there are many ways to create variety in workshops and presentations that don't require an insane amount of preparation, time, or budget.

Here's how you can start designing with contrast:

CONTRAST WITH ACTIVITIES

- Standing vs. Sitting: When facilitating workshops, I used to keep things simple and say something like, "Turn to the person next to you and share x," but I now contrast this with, "Stand up and find someone on the opposite side of the room to discuss x."

- Share the role of scribe: You don't need to be the person who does everything—share the responsibility! Plaster flipchart paper across the room and ask your participants to stand up, move around and write their thoughts on various topics on these scattered flipcharts.

- Sharing vs. reflecting: Asking the group to share their experiences or getting them to reflect individually and write their thoughts down on paper.

- Reading a manual vs. watching a video is another simple way to change your mediums.

DELIVERY TECHNIQUES

- What you say: Mix up questions, instructions, stories, and data.

- How you say it: Mix your speech pace (fast, slow, pause), pitch, and tone.

- Where you stand: Move away from your laptop's safety blanket. Present from the side of the room, the back of the room, stage left, stage right, move closer, move away. If you're on a virtual call, you can share a screen, then hide it.

- Share your voice: I use the five and one rule: I speak for no more than five minutes without introducing some contrast or giving someone else a chance to speak. Even if I just pause to allow someone to share, and check in, it adds variety, as opposed to a non-stop monologue. It's why I encourage questions throughout my session as well, as opposed to having a short amount of time at the end to answer questions. Take the question in the moment.

- Your co-facilitator: Mixing up presenters, trainers or facilitators also gives your audience a whole new experience! It also lightens the load for you and gives you a break, too.

CONTRAST IN VIRTUAL WORKSHOPS

- Use breakout rooms and small groups for role plays or mini brainstorms where participants can report back with what they learned.

- Get people to respond in Chat, or on screen.

- Switch between Gallery view, Speaker view and using digital and physical tools like my iPad, Chrome, and asking for feedback via a virtual whiteboard vs. Chat function.

- Use videos or sounds to break it up.

Andy Storch, author of *Own Your Career, Own Your Life*, shares this advice: *"One thing I do more often now as a virtual keynote speaker is to shift between showing slides and turning off slide share so that participants can see my face and sometimes each other. This gets them out of the monotony of just looking at slides the whole time, which they wouldn't necessarily be doing if they were together in person. I find this makes the sessions more engaging and interesting."* Andy is weaving in contrast through his delivery.

The key to creating contrast is incorporating unpredictability.

For example, consider how incorporating these different elements shape your next workshop:

- Standing vs. sitting

- Talking vs. listening

- Sharing vs. reflecting

- Participating vs. observing

- Reading vs. watching

- Inside vs. outside

- Loud vs. soft

- High vs. low energy

- Presenting from the front of the room vs. presenting from the back of the room, or the side (position)

- Pairs vs. groups of three

When it comes to integrating contrast into your next workshop, remember:

- You don't need to overdo it. Focus on everything in moderation instead of constant twists and turns. We want to take your audience on a journey, not a rollercoaster that they want to avoid.

- Use your SPARK Sheet to determine where contrast should go. If you scan down your workshop plan page and see you're using paired activities all the time or flipchart activities all the time, you can quickly see that you'll need to mix it up.

HERE ARE SOME ACTIVITIES

By organising your content into three primary themes, you can effectively distribute your material across these categories, dedicating roughly 25-30 minutes to each major subject area.

Now that you've plotted the topics and allocated time, your next step is to fill each slot with ideally one activity per topic that generates discussion and insight.

Pareto's Principle for Workshops: 20% of the activities listed here will give you 80% of your workshop agenda

Here are some examples of activities I use to bring content to life. Let's apply Pareto's 80/20 rule here: 20% of the activities listed here will give you 80% of your workshop agenda. I try to avoid googling any other activities.

Most of my two-hour workshop sessions for business contexts rely on this set of activities. Why? Well, a two-hour workshop is a fast session and these activities hit the mark, every time. The key is contextualising these activities in the direction of your workshop topic and the experience you're creating.

USE REAL-WORLD ACTIVITIES AND EXAMPLES (IF YOU CAN)

What is a real-life problem/opportunity they're struggling with? Overcome it together! Use the time in your session to work through it.

The most common complaint about a workshop is that it wasn't practical enough. I think that too often, we're looking for activities or ideas that simulate the challenge we're talking about. Rather than simulate the challenge, what activity can you create that is immediately applicable and helpful for your group?

Petra Zink, a Personal Brand and Digital Strategist at ImpaCCCt, deeply understands the importance of tailoring her workshops to suit her audience's context. She observes, "Often, attendees disengage because they fail to connect the learning to their own circumstances. To establish this connection, it's helpful to use analogies or language they can relate to."

For instance, Petra conducted a leadership retreat for Domino's Pizza, crafting a workshop theme revolving around the process of pizza making. Throughout the day, different "ingredients" of the pizza symbolised various workshop topics. It was an effective method to ensure that the material resonated with the group, just as pizza does!

HERE'S AN EXAMPLE:

Pat Flynn, the renowned host of the Smart Passive Income podcast, once spoke at a conference about the significance of reestablishing lost connections.

He shared an effective strategy on how to re-engage with dormant contacts in your network: The approach is simple. Take your phone, browse to the very end of your Messages app, find the oldest untouched conversation, and reignite the connection by sending a text.

During his talk, Pat didn't just share this idea; he also provided a handy script on what to say when reaching out to these old contacts.

But he didn't leave it at that. To ensure his advice wasn't just theoretical but actionable, he encouraged all the attendees to put his words into practice immediately. He asked everyone to find someone they hadn't spoken to in years and send them a text, using the script he'd just provided.

To add an element of real-time feedback, he suggested that everyone turn on their phone volumes. The following minutes were filled with the charming sounds of incoming text message alerts, proof that his re-engagement strategy was effective and immediately applicable.

WHY THIS WORKS

- It's applicable immediately.

- Your group might have a lightbulb moment as they work through the scenario or discover limitations or barriers as they get to work.

HOW TO DISCOVER THESE ACTIVITIES

Ask this guiding question: "What could we do in this session, with our time together that would be IMMEDIATELY impactful and doesn't require having to do something later?"

Remember: It's a *work*shop, not a *do-this-later*-shop.

BOB'S WORKSHOP: ACTIVITY

Framing:

We've explored Topic 1, Priorities and in front of you, you have a list of the three key things you need to work on over the next 90 days. How will you make time for that?

Instructions:

I'll invite them to open their work laptop and calendar and review:

As you look at your calendar for the next 90 days, are there activities and events that will bring you:

1. Closer to getting your top three priorities down?

2. Further away from achieving your top three priorities?

Then in groups of three, I'll ask them to:

*   Share their insights.

*   Identify three things you can schedule in your calendar right now that will get you closer to where you want to go? What are the potential barriers?

Time: I'd estimate 25-30 minutes for this activity

*   5-8 minutes individual reflection.

*   12 minutes group discussion.

*   10 minutes share back.

*   Five minutes taking action.

HELP WITH CREATING A CASE STUDY

If you need help figuring out a real activity, use a case study instead. To form a case study, refer to the conversations you held as part of your Setup stage.

Your best option is to use a real problem or opportunity for your group.

Your second-best option is to use an AI web-based tool like ChatGPT and enter a question, here's an example of a question-and-answer snippet:

Me: *I need a case study about a Supply Chain manager who is having problems finding the time to do what she needs to get done. Any ideas?*

Chat GPT: *Here's a case study:*

Meet Sarah, a supply chain manager at a fast-growing retail company. Sarah has been with the company for over five years and has built an efficient and effective supply chain system that has contributed to the company's success. However, lately, Sarah has been feeling overwhelmed with her workload and finding it hard to keep up with the demands of her job.

Sarah's days are filled with meetings, phone calls, and email correspondence, leaving her with little time to focus on strategic projects that she knows could help the company grow even further. The problem is compounded by the increasing complexity of the supply chain and the ever-changing market conditions. Sarah is feeling frustrated and stressed and is finding it hard to enjoy her job.

From this example you can ask a variety of questions that employees can explore like:

- If Sarah reported to you, what would you do?

- What should Sarah do right now? What's a longer-term approach?

- What would happen if Sarah didn't take any action?

Remember, you can edit what you receive from ChatGPT to make it more relevant for your group. I tweaked the above case study to hit the mark. Ask ChatGPT for five different examples and share with your client to see if they relate – it's a great tool to kickstart your case study.

USE QUESTIONS TO DRIVE YOUR ACTIVITY

Each of your three topic segments can really be driven by a few questions.

For example, if you're sharing project wins or insights at a lunch and learn, you can ask people at your session to reflect on a project they're working on, and how some of your project insights can apply to the way they work.

To create that contrast, all you need to do is shift the way your group responds to those prompts.

HERE ARE SOME IDEAS ON HOW TO MIX UP THE SHARE BACK/RESPONSES:

Use photo cards/stimulus

I always pack a stack of photo cards to every workshop. They're so versatile and you can use images as a prompt for a share back with questions like, *"Which photo here describes how you feel about time?"* I create my own photo cards by designing them in Canva and printing for approximately 10c Australian each.

Think-Pair-Share

This is a classic model developed by Frank Lyman, a professor at the University of Maryland, in 1981. Ask your participants to think about their responses individually, then pair them with another participant so they can share their responses. Once they've discussed it in pairs, gather a collective share back. If I'm using Zoom and want to create a think-pair-share moment, I put people in breakout rooms of at least three people. A 15-minute think-pair-share type of discussion can be very effective.

Flipchart reporting

Have different questions on walls around your room. Invite people to break into small groups and visit a flipchart. Ask them to respond to that question and after a certain period, ask them to rotate to the next flipchart and discuss that new question. Once they've rotated through all the questions, facilitate a share back of key themes.

Reverse assumptions/flip the question

The idea behind the activity is to look at a situation or problem from a different perspective by turning conventional assumptions upside down.

For example, if you were trying to solve a problem at work related to a lack of engagement among employees, the typical assumption might be that employees need more incentives or recognition to be motivated. In a reverse assumptions activity, the coach or group would challenge this assumption by flipping it on its head and considering the opposite-maybe employees would be more engaged if there were less incentives and recognition. The goal is to encourage individuals or teams to think creatively and outside the box by breaking down limiting beliefs and assumptions.

Share a story on your Best/Worst/First/Last related to your topic

Thank you to Matthew Dicks, author of *StoryWorthy* for this suggestion to prompt a share back, for example, *"Best priority, worst priority, first priority, last priority."*

MYTHBUSTER: MORE CONTENT ≠ MORE VALUE

"Before you leave the house, look in the mirror and take one thing off" - Coco Chanel

More information does not mean more value. Like a GPS, we need to cut out what's irrelevant – anything that doesn't take your group to their destination. Content overwhelm is real. We try to jam-pack sessions because we think it means more value but often, less is best.

When I was a first-time facilitator, I found myself talking an awful lot. I heard a Jim Rohn quote that stopped me in my tracks: *"How can you be so brief, yet so effective? Sometimes, we try to make up in words, what we lack in self-confidence."*

Here's an example of how my friend and client, Yoke Van Dam started transitioning her workshops from content-heavy to connection-first sessions. Yoke runs her global consultancy Y-Connect, from South Africa, where she is a leadership and sales expert. When she first started delivering workshops, she felt she was there to speak and pass on a message. In her own words, she thought she was disconnected from her group. With good intentions, she wanted to give as much value as possible, jam-packing content into slide after slide.

Up to that point, she always relied on mostly PowerPoint slides and PowerPoint handouts in her sessions. She discovered through our work together that group discussions and implementation were much more important than simply relaying content.

This gave Yoke freedom: She could plan out the activities and then drop them if they ended up taking longer than anticipated and not make the group feel as if they missed out on something.

She then added contrast through movement, games, music, and flipchart work but also mixed it up with individual solo work, pair work or group work. She started adding more activities and often didn't even use workbooks.

These days, she wakes up to emails from clients, sharing things like:

- *"Yoke exceeded our expectations by going beyond the 'how-to's."*

- *"Awesome informative event! Really inspirational!"*

- *"My mind was blown away."*

Yoke discovered that less content and more focused activity and discussion helped boost the experience for her groups.

Now we've identified that mixing up activities, questions and share back rounds is important, let's see add that detail to our SPARK Sheet.

BOB'S WORKSHOP: ACTIVITY SECTION OUTLINE

Timing	Topic	Tools
09:20	**Activities** Topic One: Priorities • Bob: Provide clarity on the next 90 days • Outline three things your team is working towards	• Bob briefing • Individual reflection and share as group.
09:45	Topic Two: Discipline Forming and maintaining boundaries • Calendar reflection • Scripts and group coaching	• Calendar review activity • Group coaching: Methods to build relationships while staying firm.
10:10	Topic 3: Tech and systems to help you speed up. • How to automate some processes	Share screen: • Time-blocking • Template responses

CHECKPOINT

• Reflect on the last workshop you attended. What activities or techniques did the facilitator use that you found engaging and could implement in your own workshops?

• How can you use real-world activities and examples in your sessions? Write down a list of possible scenarios or problems that could be solved collaboratively during a workshop.

• Think about the ways you use questions to drive your activities. Are they effective in sparking discussion and insight? If not, what could you change?

ACT

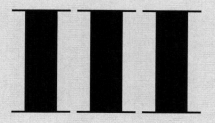

Put the finishing touches to your SPARK Sheet, wrapping up your two-hour workshop design. But the workshop isn't over when it's over. Across the next two chapters, you'll identify questions and activities to close your workshop, and strategies to communicate more value to your participants once it's finished.

CHAPTER EIGHT

R is for Review

CHAPTER SUMMARY

Congratulations on making it to the Review part of your workshop! I think you'll find your two-hour workshop goes by incredibly quickly. It's sad, but all workshops must come to an end. That's how you want your group to feel by the end: *"It's over? Nooooo!"*

YOU'LL LEARN THE FOLLOWING:

- A cool-down sequence you can use to close every workshop.

- A variety of questions you can use for a share-back round.

YOU'LL WALK AWAY WITH THE FOLLOWING:

- A completed Review section in your SPARK Sheet.

The Review section is the final part of your workshop, where your participants reflect on key insights and actions. It's also an opportunity for you to understand what was most valuable.

DO:

- Give your Review section more time than you anticipate.

- Remember how you want your group to feel by the end of the session so that you can direct the energy.

DON'T:

- Skip the Review part.

- Let your workshop go on longer than the planned end time.

- Drag your session out to make the end time: You have permission to end your session early.

The recency effect is a psychological phenomenon where the most recent information is more likely to be remembered and significantly impacts people's thoughts and behaviours. A strong conclusion can help reinforce the learning that has taken place throughout the workshop and maximise its impact.

KNOW YOUR ROLE: YOU CAN'T CONTROL ANY ACTION (OR LACK THEREOF) TAKEN AFTER YOUR WORKSHOP

> *"A real decision is measured by the fact that you've taken a new action. If there's no action, you haven't truly decided"*
> *- Tony Robbins*

As I've grown older and more pragmatic about workshops and training sessions, I've accepted that we can only control and influence what's being done in the room. It took me a while to realise this, but it's not our job to *make* our participants change their behaviour. Our role as workshop hosts and facilitators is to build awareness, hopefully, get people excited about a topic, and inspired to do something. But after that? It's on them. This is a responsibility that participants need to own.

Our environment and habits are a remarkable predictor of how we will behave. Knowing this, what we can do to gain some influence is to allocate time within our sessions to help inspire some tiny actions.

CREATE YOUR END OF WORKSHOP RITUAL

It helps to have a closing sequence that you can rely on. Here's my end of workshop ritual:

1. Address the Parking Lot.

2. Ask a reflection question.

3. Generate a share-back round.

4. Prompts to continue the conversation.

5. Say bye!

1. Address the Parking Lot

It's essential to ensure that anything raised during the workshop, either before it starts or during the session, is acknowledged and addressed in some way. If you don't know the answer, it's okay to say, "I'm not sure", or" I'll send that to you later."

- Check in to see what questions remain outstanding. This is also a great time to see if any new questions pop up. Your options are:

  o Answer the question in the session (the best option).

  o If you can't, take a note and advise on how you'll progress it by either escalating the question to someone else or taking action to respond. Note: If you take any of these options, make sure you follow up, your job is to increase trust.

- Collecting the Parking Lot can be done by having a flipchart or a digital document to capture these outstanding items.

2. Ask a reflection question

Here are some questions you can ask to solicit key insights or action from your group:

- What are you committing to do moving forward? What action can you take right now, to make that happen?

- What are 1-2 key things you learned today?

- What's one thing you learned about someone else?

- What's one insight you had today?

- How has your thinking changed because of today's session?

- What tools or resources do you need to continue to grow and develop?

- How will you measure your success in applying what you learned?

- What obstacles might you face in implementing what you learned, and how will you overcome them?

- Who can you reach out to for support as you implement what you learned?

- What resources or communities can you join to stay connected and continue learning?

- What support do you need from others in this room to help you implement what you learned?

If you'd like to add some spin to your questions, here are other ways to ask for reflection:

- What's the tweetable for you? (280 characters or less.)

- What hashtag would describe what you learned in this session?

- What do you want to stop/start/continue?

BOB'S WORKSHOP: REVIEW

I'm using my three key topics as inspiration for the reflection question.

I'll ask: *"Which area requires most of your focus: Priority, Discipline or System? What's a tiny action you can take to move in this direction?"*

I love this question because it reinforces the underpinning three key topics.

Timing	Topic	Tools
10:35	**Review:** Which area requires most of your focus: Priority, Discipline or System? What's a tiny action you can take to move in this direction?	• Think-pair-share
11 am	Close	

3. Generate a share-back round

First consider how many people you have in your session.

- If you have fewer than seven participants, you can go around and check everyone out/see what they thought in less than two minutes.

  o Round the room: Ask each person to share and progress along clockwise/anti-clockwise.

  o Ball Toss: Participants stand in a circle and throw a ball to each other while sharing one thing they learned or liked about the workshop. All participants stand back, or sit once they have shared, so they can see who is left to share. Or if it's virtual they can post a reaction so we know who already shared.

o   Virtually, try the 'handover' round where someone in your group responds and they're responsible for picking the next person to share.

• If there are more than seven people, maybe avoid an individual share-back round in a two-hour workshop because it consumes too much time.

o   One way to capture the share back is through a group check-in and report-back, or you can ask a few people to share if they feel comfortable doing so.

o   There are tools like Slido, or collaborative software like Google Docs, where people can add their reflections or insights, and of course, if you're leading this virtually, you can capture it in the Chat box.

o   Mind Map: Participants work together to create a mind map of the key takeaways from the workshop.

o   Speed Sharing: Participants pair up and have a few minutes to share one thing they learned with their partner.

4. Prompts to continue the conversation

Here are some important details you can include on a slide that shows how people can connect with you after the workshop; these ideas mainly apply to external facilitators or consultants:

- Contact information: Email address and social media handles.

- Website: Include a link to a specific page if you're offering free resources (ideally, they need to enter their email address to get your resources), using a QR code might help, too. Resources could include a checklist or even a copy of your visuals if you used any.

- Encouragement to connect: End with a friendly and approachable message encouraging participants to connect with you after the workshop. I'll always say, *"Let's continue the conversation!"* I genuinely enjoy hearing from people after my sessions, and I always encourage connection.

- Reminder of what you need them to do, if anything.

Energised ways to end:

- Turn to each other and say, "You're awesome."

- Round of applause.

- Play some great music.

- Group photo: Encourage participants to take a group photo to commemorate their experience.

"THAT WAS PRETTY USEFUL"

You don't need to facilitate a life-changing moment, but a slight degree pivot in their thinking can create a tremendous ripple effect.

Make several decisions upfront and ensure you have allocated enough time in your SPARK Sheet:

- Do you want people contacting you directly or will they go through your client?

- Will you stick around to answer questions after? Or do you have to duck out?

- Do you need to buffer time for things like group photos?

IT'S OKAY TO FINISH YOUR SESSION A LITTLE EARLY. JUST DON'T FINISH IT LATE!

If you have extra time, wrap up a minute or two before the scheduled end time. Give the gift of time! It's better to end the workshop confidently rather than letting it linger on awkwardly in silence. If participants have more questions or want to continue the discussion, they can connect with you later.

If you feel more discussion is required, and you're happy to extend, use a phrase like: "We're getting close to the top of the hour, and I understand there are some more questions and comments. I'm happy to stick around for a few extra minutes. However, if you have to go, that's fine; thank you for being here."

If you finished very early and need some backup ideas:

- Review key points: You could use the extra time to review the key points covered in the workshop, reinforcing the main takeaways, and answering any remaining questions.

- Go over additional material: If you had planned to cover more material but ran out of time, you could use the extra 20 minutes to delve deeper into a topic.

- Engage in a group activity: You could use the extra time to do a group activity that helps participants apply what they learned in the workshop. This could be something as simple as a brainstorming session or a role-playing exercise.

- Ask for feedback: You could use the extra time to ask participants for feedback on the workshop, soliciting their thoughts on what worked well and what could be improved. This can help you tailor future workshops better to meet the needs and preferences of your participants.

- Factor more time into your Review stage. It's a great opportunity to hear key insights, plan or take tiny actions and get insightful feedback to improve your workshops, too.

CHECKPOINT

- Consider how you might handle a share-back round in both small and large groups. What methods or tools would you use to ensure everyone has a chance to share?

- Design your own end of workshop ritual. What activities or questions would you include to wrap up effectively?

- Consider the potential obstacles participants might face when trying to implement what they've learned. How can you address these during the Review section?

CHAPTER NINE

K is for Keep

CHAPTER SUMMARY

One of the most popular questions I receive is, "How do I keep the magic going long after the workshop?" It's nice to prepare your workshop after-party and send through some essential resources. After running a killer workshop, the last thing I want to do is trudge home and create a document full of resources. So, I typically set mine up in advance.

YOU'LL LEARN THE FOLLOWING:

- The importance of providing a summary of the workshop and relevant resources to retain the information and insights acquired during the session.

- The benefits of creating workshop show notes to provide value to participants.

YOU'LL WALK AWAY WITH:

- A completed SPARK Sheet. Success!

Let's explore various ways to wrap up your workshop, share follow-up materials, gather feedback, and offer additional resources to your participants. Speed matters in this process, so plan before the workshop starts. Discover various strategies to summarise the workshop, share follow-up materials and gather feedback.

DO:

- Follow up with what you promised within 24 hours of your session.

- Set up resource guides/go-to's so you don't need to reinvent the wheel.

DON'T:

- Throw away your SPARK Sheet.

SPEED MATTERS

Before you even start your workshop, have a plan in place for what you'll share with your participants after the session. This will help you move quickly and efficiently, ensuring that your resources are sent out while the workshop is still fresh in everyone's minds.

CREATE WORKSHOP SHOW NOTES

One way to provide value to your participants is by creating workshop show notes. For a podcast, show notes are shared for each episode highlighting books/articles/tools mentioned in the conversation. The same concept can be applied to your workshop. List all the mentioned resources and link to relevant articles, books, and other resources. You can create a Google Doc or a private page on your website to store these resources.

I can typically anticipate which resources I'll share in a workshop. I often recommend some of my favourite books, so I have some templates available in Notion and on my website (unlisted links).

I'll add great podcast conversations to a playlist when I hear them. I created a leadership podcast playlist on Spotify, where I've captured some of my favourite insights. I'll share this Spotify playlist in the show notes if I'm hosting a leadership-related workshop. You can also create specific playlists on YouTube to cover any of your workshop topic themes. Such resources, once created, can consistently serve as a treasure trove of value for your future groups.

If you can't access your participants directly, use this statement when you share it with your client: *"I'm following up on our meeting with your staff yesterday—they wanted some further resources, and I'm forwarding this list for you to distribute."*

Aim to send this through within 24 hours while the conversations remain fresh. Include group photos! There's a chance these could be shared on their organisation's Yammer site or LinkedIn. Read through the Chat conversations to discover if any questions or prompts could be used to kickstart a follow-up conversation with your client or give you new workshop ideas.

One effective way to mitigate the effects of the forgetting curve is to encourage participants to take notes and review them later. Another is to have participants create an action plan or set goals for themselves, which helps embed the learning into their minds. Additionally, following up with participants after the workshop through emails, check-ins, or even a follow-up session, can help reinforce the information and ensure that it's retained over time.

FEEDBACK FORMS: GATHERING FEEDBACK AND ASKING WHAT ELSE THEY NEED

If you're sharing a feedback form, it's a good idea to combine getting feedback with asking what else they need.

Sometimes, having a physical version of this can increase your chances of getting a response, for example, having a postcard and asking them to provide their details, and answer tick-box questions.

For digital surveys, platforms include Survey Monkey or Google Forms. Include a QR on your slides, directing them to complete it.

In the resources in this book, I've shared an example of a Google Forms template you can duplicate and personalise for your session.

Questions can include:

• What did you hope to hear more about that wasn't covered?

• What was covered that was most valuable?

- How would you describe [facilitator name] and his/her/their session to others? [May I quote you on that? Yes/No]

- Would you like to have [facilitator name] back in future? If so, which topics would most be of interest? [list topics below]

- Would you like [facilitator name] to contact you about any of the following services? [include the other services you deliver]

- Their contact details.

- Ask them to opt in for information about future sessions. See example below:

Example: Opt in for information about future sessions

To stay up to date with our latest sessions and workshops, you can opt in to receive email notifications.

Simply check the box below and give us your express consent to receive our emails.

[ ] Yes, I would like to be notified when new sessions and workshops are available.

Promote your great work

- If you have permission, share a photo of you / the venue / pre-, during or post-workshop on LinkedIn, along with a caption that captures any insights from your session.

Do the same thing with Instagram Stories (if your target audience is on IG).

One of the best books I've never read is Dr Wayne Dyer's *It's never crowded along the extra mile.* The great thing about keeping your essential tools and resources organised in one place is that it conveys the impression of going above and beyond, while being efficient and smart with using your resources from previous sessions. Most importantly, keep the SPARK framework front of mind when you start workshopping your next session.

REPURPOSE YOUR EFFORTS

Maximise the impact of your sessions with the SPARK Sheet. After each session, take a few moments to reflect and annotate your experiences, noting the effectiveness of each activity and topic. Keep all your annotated sheets in a handy display folder for easy access in the future. For added convenience, consider setting up an online version, using tools like SessionLab.com or organising them in a digital catalogue using Notion.

There's no point reinventing the wheel. No matter how you choose to store your SPARK Sheets, they will serve as a valuable resource and source of inspiration for future workshops.

Success! Here's the completed SPARK Sheet for Bob's session.

SETUP	
Workshop title: We've got this: Refocus for the next 90 days. **Mini-Mission Statement:** This workshop is for senior leaders in the Supply Chain team who are working long hours and not feeling like they're making traction towards their department's goals. They want to refocus their energy to hit their top three targets in the next 90 days. **Session Vibe:** Create a calm, "I've got this" feeling in the room **Location/Time:** The Awesome Room, 9 am start (room booked for 8 am)	**Prep:** Pre-video announcing two things: Pre-Survey and What to Bring **Pre-survey:** What's getting in the way of you achieving your Q1 priorities? **Prep:** Work calendar (digital or paper planner is fine)

Timing	Topic	Tools
08:30	**Power Up**: Have the following ready by 08:30 am • Flipchart stand, pre-prepared flipchart and pens. • Post-its and highlighters on table	• PowerPoint slideshow with quotes related to time memes, quotes, and questions on the screen

09:00	• Introduction:
	  o Welcome
	  o Calendar Tetris story: Doesn't it feel like you're trying to fill in blocks of time every day, but you're still not winning?
	  o Overview of the session: Ask Bob to share why he requested this session.
	  o Personal introduction (keep it short, 90 seconds max)
	  o Objections/Scope clarification
	• Logistics:
	  o Ask questions anytime!
	  o Housekeeping is not required as they all work together in the same office.
	• Buckle-up approach
	  o Priorities
	  o Discipline
	  o Systems
	• Strongest/Improve? Individually reflect and share back
		• Flipchart + pen to draw Venn diagram.
		• Paired discussion

09:20	**Activities** Topic 1: Where are you going? • Bob: Provide clarity on the next 90 days • Outline three things your team is working towards	• Bob briefing • Individual reflection and share as group
09:45	Topic 2: Forming and maintaining boundaries. • Calendar reflection • Scripts and group coaching	• Calendar review activity • Group coaching: Methods to build relationships while staying firm
10:10	Topic 3: Tech and systems to help you speed up	Share screen: • Time-blocking • Template responses
10:35	**Review:** Which area requires most of your focus: Priority, Discipline or System? What's a tiny action you can take to move in this direction?	• Think-pair-share
11 am	**Close**	

Keep
Send a link with key resources (use an existing Notion page). Schedule a 30 min check-in with Bob.

As you can see in the Keep section, I'll duplicate an existing Notion page I created earlier which already has my favourite resources in it. You can see what mine looks like by accessing all the tools at 2hourwork.shop/freebies.

I've also scheduled a check-in with Bob to determine if we hit the workshop aims, and if there are any opportunities to help in future. Remember, a workshop is one of many tools to help get a result.

CHECKPOINT

- What are some specific resources you've found helpful after attending a workshop or seminar?

- Create a list of potential resources you might share after a future workshop you're planning.

- Complete your SPARK Sheet by finalising your Keep section.

As you glance through it, how does it feel? Make it your own. If you feel like you need to add more detail, like questions under each Activity to have as a back-pocket measure, include them.

Your SPARK Sheet needs to help you build your confidence. Add the detail it requires to make you feel like you've got this!

ENCORE

OUR MISSION AND NEXT STEPS

Congrats! This marks the beginning of your journey into a captivating and rewarding career. You don't need to label yourself as a facilitator or trainer to share your knowledge and host memorable group experiences. Hosting events and leading group discussions are valuable skills that can take you to exciting places and connect you with remarkable people.

A major theme in this guide was trying to help you stop the curve of overthinking. It's so easy to want to endlessly search to find the perfect activity. However, when you focus on the challenges and opportunities that your target group currently faces, the ideal workshop activities become more apparent.

Remember, the goal is to find effective solutions, not to strive for unattainable perfection.

I hope this book has helped you bust through some limiting beliefs, making workshop design and delivery accessible for you, and given you some ideas you can try in your next session.

LET'S STAMP OUT BORING WORKSHOPS, FOREVER.

If you think others could benefit from *The 2-Hour Workshop Blueprint*, I would be grateful for your help in any way:

- Rate and/or write a review on Amazon (the fastest way to an author's heart is through an Amazon review!)

- Gift a copy to a friend, or your team.

- Share your insights by taking photos of your workshops-in-progress and tagging me on social media or using the hashtag #2hrworkshop.

- Tune in to the *First Time Facilitator* podcast, where I interview workshop hosts all around the world, and ask them how they make their sessions amazing.

THANK YOU FOR READING

It's party time! If you love the two-hour time frame, you might enjoy Nick Gray's book, *The 2-Hour Cocktail Party*. His book inspired this book; I loved how it was so actionable, structured, and specific.

I'd love to know how you go with designing your workshops. I would be thrilled to connect with you on all the social media platforms, and please send me an email at hello@leannehughes. com, on how you're creating amazing punchy workshop experiences.

APPENDICES

Helpful Extras

The Helpful Extras Chapter includes some fun things outside of the SPARK framework to help you improve your workshop experience.

Dig into some handy bonus content, including:

- **A: Executive Summary** – A compact overview to get you started.

- **B: Countdown Calendar** – A strategic timeline to optimise your preparation.

- **C: Favourite Workshop Tech Tools** – Harness the power of technology to streamline your workshop.

- **D: How to Manage Behaviour and Deal with the Unknown** – Pro tips to handle unexpected situations and maintain a positive workshop environment.

- **E: How to Transition Between Topics** – Master the art of seamless transitions to maintain engagement.

A: EXECUTIVE SUMMARY

To design and host your two-hour workshop, follow the SPARK framework:

- **Setup:** We're not just ticking boxes here; we're crafting an experience. Get clear on your audience, understand their needs, and wants, and start connecting with your group before the session has started. This isn't about pushing content; it's about creating meaning.

- **Power Up:** Light up the room, set the rhythm and expectations, and start the conversation upfront. We're here to engage, excite and empower.

- **Activities:** Design activities that are more than fillers—they're the main event. Align them with the workshop's goals, encourage active participation and let the conversation flow. This is where the magic happens.

- **Review:** We're not closing the book; we're reflecting on the story. What did we learn? How will we apply it? Let's debrief, discuss next steps, provide feedback, and evaluate our journey as a workshop host.

- **Keep:** Who said the conversation must stop when the clock does? Follow up, provide resources, and keep the dialogue alive. Take a moment to pat yourself on the back, but don't forget to identify areas for growth. And don't forget to save those gold-star activities for next time.

B: COUNTDOWN CALENDAR

Note: This is an ideal way to create your workshop in a way that reduces your stress, keeping in mind that sometimes you may not have the luxury of two weeks to prepare; in that case, condense these steps.

Two Weeks Before

- Identify why a workshop is required: Get a clear understanding of who will be attending the workshop.

- Craft the experience: Design workshop content that is meaningful and impactful for the audience.

- Start connecting: Send out pre-workshop material and a welcome note to all participants to help them prepare and get excited about the workshop.

One Week Before

- Map the three key overarching topics and themes that will help get your group the result they're after.

- Finalise your activities: Confirm your activities and exercises align with the workshop's objectives.

- Reminder: Send out a reminder email to the group (you might like to include a video) so they know what to expect.

One Day Before

- Prep your materials: Ensure all your materials, whether digital or physical, are ready.

- Tech check: Do a run-through of any tech platforms or tools you'll be using.

◊ Mental prep: Take some time for yourself to rest and mentally prepare for the workshop and iron your shirt the night before!

On the Day

- Check-in: Arrive early to the venue or log in early if it's a virtual workshop. Do any last-minute checks.

- Welcome: As participants arrive, welcome them, and set a positive tone for the day.

First 15 Minutes

- Set the stage: Reiterate the workshop goals.

- Buckle-up: Kick off with a conversation and questions primed to connect your group with the content immediately.

Last 15 Minutes

- Debrief: Conduct a debriefing session, discussing what was learned and the next steps.

- Feedback: Encourage participants to provide feedback on the workshop.

Within 24 Hours

- Follow-up: Send out a thank you email to all participants, along with any post-workshop resources, and a summary of what was covered.

- Reflection: Take some time to reflect on the workshop's successes and areas for improvement. Record these for future reference so you don't need to reinvent the wheel the next time you host.

C: FAVOURITE WORKSHOP TECH TOOLS

For the latest version of this list and links to tools, visit 2hourwork. shop/freebies.

Software	Description	SPARK Application
ChatGPT	ChatGPT is a conversational AI that can understand and generate human-like text based on the context of the conversation. It's great for workshops as a brainstorming buddy and can serve as a virtual assistant, helping to answer participants' queries, provide information, and even assist with scheduling and reminders.	Setup: Respond to queries and provide information. Activities: Help with formulating case studies and finding articles that support your information. Keep: Assist with follow-up communication.

Descript	An audio and video editing software that uses AI, Descript lets you edit media files like a text document, making it perfect for pre and post-workshop video content creation or editing recordings of your workshop. It also has transcription and overdub features, enhancing accessibility for your participants.	Power Up: Edit and share your pre-workshop video message. Keep: Create accessible materials for post-workshop review.
Google Forms	This tool allows you to create custom surveys, quizzes, and feedback forms. It's great for collecting pre- and post-workshop information, and post-workshop feedback. Responses are compiled in an easy-to-analyse format.	Setup: Collect pre-workshop information. Review: Gather post-workshop feedback.
Nearpod	An interactive presentation and assessment tool that can be used to create engaging workshops. Nearpod allows you to create interactive slides that can include quizzes, polls, and videos, and you can monitor participation in real-time.	Power Up: Present workshop introduction and goals. Activities: Engage participants with interactive slides. Review: Assess learning with quizzes and polls.
Notion	An all-in-one workspace where you can write, plan, collaborate, and organise. Notion is excellent for workshops as it can be used to plan your workshop structure, keep track of participant information, create checklists, and store all your workshop materials in one place.	Setup: Plan workshop structure and keep track of participant information. Activities: Share workshop materials. Keep: Store records and materials for future reference.

Slido	An audience interaction tool, Slido lets you create polls, collect questions, and gather feedback in real-time during your workshop. It can increase participation and make your workshop more dynamic and interactive.	Power Up: Collect initial questions or ice breaker responses. Activities: Run real-time polls. Review: Gather immediate feedback.
Spotify	This digital music streaming service provides access to millions of songs and podcasts. It's fantastic for workshops as you can create custom playlists to set the mood during activities or breaks, or even use educational podcasts as part of your workshop material.	Power Up: Play energising music to set the mood. Activities: Stream background music (just beware of copyright).
VideoAsk	VideoAsk allows you to have asynchronous video conversations making it great for personalised interactions. It's perfect for pre-workshop introductions or gathering video testimonials post-workshop.	Setup: Use for pre-workshop introductions. Review: Gather video testimonials. Keep: Use for follow-up Q&As.
YouTube	YouTube is a vast video-sharing platform that can serve as a valuable resource for workshops. Moreover, if you're recording your workshops, YouTube can be a great platform for archiving and sharing these recordings with your participants.	Setup: Share instructional videos. Activities: Showcase relevant content. Keep: Archive and share workshop recordings; create a YouTube playlist for yourself of videos that are worth storing for future sessions.
Zoom	Zoom offers seamless audio and video communication, along with features like breakout rooms and whiteboards.	Power Up: Use for virtual workshops. Activities: Use breakout rooms for group activities.

D: HOW TO MANAGE BEHAVIOUR AND DEAL WITH THE UNKNOWN

Countless things can happen during your two-hour workshop. Instead of worrying about the 1% chance of rare problems, let's address the most common workshop challenges:

- Unresponsive participants
- Overly dominant participants
- Late workshop start
- Venue changes
- Zoom link issues
- Technical difficulties

FIRST THINGS FIRST

When faced with unexpected situations, create space to respond calmly. Maintain composure and project confidence while addressing the issue.

Keep the group informed. There might be someone in the group who can help with what's happening. Determine if you should call a break or move your session start time.

Avoid over-apologising. One apology, or an announcement like, "*Thank you for your patience*" is enough; step into solution mode.

PLAN FOR YOUR TECH TO FAIL

For in-person workshops, use technology to enhance content, but don't rely on it. That creates a sense of freedom. I had a situation in Singapore where my MacBook could not link up to a conference room's data projector. I felt a sense of freedom when I realised, I didn't need those slides. I had my SPARK Sheet printed and in front of me, and I could run the workshop following the ideas captured there.

For virtual sessions:

- Assign a co-host to keep the session running if you're disconnected.

- Know how to contact your group (email, Slack, Teams) to provide updates.

- Test technology beforehand, especially with platforms like Microsoft Teams (which has weird access rights that change, depending on your role within an organisation).

MANAGING ENGAGEMENT

You've done all you can to prepare right but you still can't eliminate these scenarios:

- Unresponsive or hesitant participants.

- Dominant participants not allowing others to speak.

For hesitant participants:

- Encourage individual reflection before responding.

- Use pair-sharing or small group discussions.

- Provide focused prompts for output, "What two key themes did your group discuss?" provides more focus, instead of asking "What did you discuss?"

To keep sessions on track, use phrases like:

- Say, *"Can we have one conversation so everyone can hear everyone's great points,"* and then invite the ones who are talking to share one at a time.

- Interrupt by asking, *"I'll just have to jump in and pause you here."* or *"We're hearing a lot of great ideas from this side of the room, how about the other side?"*

- Use body language: Hover near the two people who are talking to each other while you're presenting to deter side conversations.

SCENARIO

Imagine you're hosting a virtual workshop and one of your guests, Cassandra, continues to respond to your questions negatively, also taking up space and not allowing others in your session to contribute.

Two questions:

1. *What will happen if you let Cassandra continue and you don't intervene?*

2. *If you decide you need to respond, what do you do?*

If your goal is to hear all voices and that's not happening, you need to intervene. Your group is looking to you for that leadership to balance time and voices.

Some helpful phrases to get your conversation back on track include:

- *"Thanks for sharing your story; we're limited with time. Would you mind sharing your #1 tip?"*

- *"That's a terrific point! It reminds me / is different to a time when…"[segue back to main topic].*

- *"Given how much time we have, I'm going to have to move this conversation along."*

- *"It's great we're talking about this specific topic. However, I think this may only apply to a small number of people in this room. How about we broaden the conversation to include [restate the purpose of your workshop]?"*

HANDLE CONFLICTING OPINIONS

- Allow discussions to unfold, asking for other views.

- Assess if the conversation is relevant to the workshop objective.

- Use the group's input to guide the conversation: *"Is this the conversation we need to have in order to [workshop objective]"* when done well, asking the group for guidance and direction is a host's superpower.

- Redirect off-topic discussions (*"I committed to having everyone leave on time."*) or park ideas for later.

Naturally, the way you convey your message is just as crucial as the content itself—your delivery significantly impacts its effectiveness. When introducing one of these phrases, adopt a lower, more authoritative tone while maintaining a friendly demeanour.

REMEMBER: IT'S NOT ALL ON YOU

Despite our inability to foresee every hurdle during a workshop, meticulous preparation in the Setup phase can significantly reduce potential issues.

Additionally, I want to reassure you of an inescapable reality when it comes to hosting workshops: Even if you perform exceptionally well, it's impossible to satisfy everyone. When working with a diverse group, it's essential to remember that not all responsibility should fall on your shoulders. Accepting this fact is one of the most challenging aspects of our roles.

E: HOW TO TRANSITION BETWEEN TOPICS

When I interviewed Michael Bungay Stanier on the *First Time Facilitator* podcast, he said that new facilitators should strive to be barely adequate, and that you should focus on your content, your energy and how to transition between topics.

Groups can roam far from the original agenda and may require guidance to return to the workshop intention, this is where it helps to be able to transition between topics.

Transitions come in two forms:

1. Obvious transitions

2. Seamless transitions

1. Obvious transitions

Tim Ferriss, in his podcast, employs phrases like the following to transition topics:

- *"Let's take a sharp left turn"*: Example: We're discussing productivity, and now let's abruptly shift to candle-making—not every transition must be smooth.

- *"Let's double-click that!"*: An invitation to delve deeper into the topic.

Alternatively, you can use segues, like a newsreader, for topic transitions. Segues help guide the conversation in a new direction that aligns with your workshop's focus and objectives.

2. Seamless transitions

The Australian TV show *The Chasers* featured a segment called "Seamless Segues", showcasing newsreaders skilfully transitioning between unrelated news stories.

Here's a segue example connecting drink driving to fruit juice: *"Karen Cooper just reported on alcohol excess. Speaking of excess, did you know fruit juice can also be deadly according to recent research?"*

Breakdown: A common descriptor (excess) was used to bridge the gap between drink driving and excessive fruit juice consumption.

Another for instance, connecting Paris with bananas: *"Paris is famous for its scrumptious croissants, which are almost as delightful as the bananas growing in my backyard."*

Linking phrase: Almost as delightful

While hosting workshops, search for a connecting word or phrase to smoothly transition to the next topic. With practice, you'll be able to link any subject to your workshop's central theme.

To hone your transitioning skills, employ brainstorming techniques like Forced Connections. This method sparks innovative ideas by merging two seemingly unrelated concepts or objects.

FORCED CONNECTIONS: A CREATIVE TECHNIQUE

(Adapted from authors Don Koberg and Jim Bagnal)

Objective: Encourage innovative thinking by identifying connections between seemingly unrelated items or ideas.

Consider the example of Paris and Bananas. Create two columns, listing attributes or associations for each item:

Paris	Banana
Eiffel Tower	Yellow
Beautiful	Grows on a plant
Romantic	Delicious
Bridges	Healthy
Croissants	High in potassium
Mona Lisa	Tropical fruit

In this case, we can find a connection through the word 'delicious' linked to croissants. Alternatively, we could force a connection by stating, "Tropical weather is rare in Paris, making banana growth unlikely. Speaking of bananas..."

While this step-by-step breakdown is useful for understanding the technique, it's essential to practice Forced Connections regularly to develop the skill of making connections on-the-fly during workshops. Also, the Forced Connections activity is an excellent tool for stimulating creative thinking that you can use during the Activities stage.

ACKNOWLEDGEMENTS

B ig thanks to Jenny Blake, who kickstarted this whole project when she sent me a voice note saying, *"Leanne! You've had over 200 conversations about facilitation. I feel like you need to write a book about workshops!"*

Huge props to my dad, Aneurin Hughes, who has been so helpful along the way, providing detailed feedback, constant encouragement, and great ideas on bringing this to life.

If you love the illustrations, make sure you connect with Jade Miller (https://jademiller.com.au/). She's super talented at drawing, making you laugh and structuring ideas.

Shout-outs to:

- My mentor, Alan Weiss, who can design impactful two-day workshops in five minutes.

- Andy Storch, for inviting me to speak at his Talent Development Think Tank conference in California; that conference was the impetus for getting this book together.

- Shout-out to Dave Foxall, editor extraordinaire! It's great to work with people who are so good with an eye for detail, patience, and a sense of humour.

- This amazing core group of friends who commented on Version 1 of this book fron front to back, while also sharing their workshop expertise:

    o **Steph Clarke**, Reimagining learning at work at 28 Thursdays and podcast host of Steph's Business Bookshelf

    o **Jan Keck**, Creator of Ask Deep Questions, and soon-to-be-author of Ice Melters

    o **Dr Cathryn Lloyd** from Maverick Minds and author: The Story Cookbook, Facilitation with Stories and Seriously Playful Creativity

    o **Antonio Iturra Novoa**, Visual facilitator and specialist in collaboration, innovation and creativity, creator of Collaborative Offerings method

    o **Rachel Okazaki,** CEO, ATypical Physical Therapy and Wellness, Owner/Creative Director at The Hangry Moose

    o **Prina Shah** from Prina Shah Consulting and podcast host of Ways to Change the Workplace

Workshop Wingmates

Thank you for being part of this group, or sharing your feedback and thoughts during the writing process!

Jo Alilovic, Steven Bleistein, Mireille Beumer, Brad Callanan, Kate Crawshaw, Leanne Elliott, Thomas Fry, Dee Gagnon, Jason Latimer, Sean Lavin, Ashleigh Loughnan, Jasmine Malki, Eleanor McNeil, Hughes Mileng, Kate Munro, Tomoo Okubo, Rhonda Rosborough, Nicole Salter, Joeri Schilders, Jeff Skipper, Tom Scantlebury, Douglas Squirrel, Juan Daniel Sobrado, Gosia Syta, Penny Tainton and Bethan Winn.

And finally, lots of love to Quincey and Milo, who were by my side, sitting under the desk as I was drafting these ideas up. Thank you, Chris, for your encouragement and support while I spoke about the book process, endlessly.

I've posted a full list of thanks with links and photos at 2hourwork.shop/thanks.

TINY ASK!

THANKS A TON FOR READING MY BOOK!

I really appreciate all your feedback and I love hearing what you have to say.

I need your help to make this book and my future books even better.

Could you take just ninety seconds to write a review on Amazon sharing your thoughts?

Here's the link: 2hourwork.shop/review

Thank you!

- Leanne Hughes

END CREDITS: ADDITIONAL RESOURCES FOR WORKSHOP HOSTS

There are many tools to support you in implementing *The 2-Hour Workshop Blueprint*:

- The Flipchart Facebook group: Join thousands of workshop hosts sharing their ideas and questions. Search for *The Flipchart* on Facebook.

- Sign up to my newsletter: I share behind the scenes, fresh ideas, and the latest updates over at: leannehughes.com/subscribe.

- Join the Booked Out Facilitator program: If you want to take the skill of workshop hosting pro, and learn how to book out five more workshops for every workshop you deliver, visit bookedoutfacilitator.com.

- Subscribe to the *First Time Facilitator* podcast: Learn how to create unpredictable workshop experiences (that predictably work): firsttimefacilitator.com.

- All the resources for this book are at: 2hourwork.shop/freebies.

THE 2-HOUR WORKSHOP BLUEPRINT
FOR ORGANISATIONS

Scalable rollout options for conferences, training teams and large organisations include:

- Interactive keynote, webinars and workshops for employees and managers.

- Consulting projects, where I help you build your work cultures, spark connections, and redesign your programs and events.

- The 2-Hour Workshop Blueprint and Virtual Train-the-Trainer certification and licensing.

Say hi and reach out hello@leannehughes.com.

I can't wait to work(shop) with you!

Printed in Great Britain
by Amazon

29867031R00104